Living In

SOUTH
KOREA

ROB WHYTE
KYOUNG-MI KIM

Second Edition

PRO LINGUA  ASSOCIATES

Pro Lingua Associates, Publishers

P.O. Box 1348
Brattleboro, Vermont 05302-1348 USA
Office: 802 257 7779
Orders: 800 366 4775
E-mail: Info@ProLinguaAssociates.com
Webstore: http://www.ProLinguaAssociates.com
SAN: 216-0579

ISBN 0-86647-222-3

This book follows the general format of the *Living In* series originally developed by The Experiment in International Living, now known as World Learning, in Brattleboro, Vermont, as part of its Orientation Development Project. Peter deJong, former Secretary General, and the directors of the various Experiment in International Living National Offices identified the original content areas covered in this country-specific series. The initial development funds were provided by the U. S. Information Agency under the President's International Youth Initiative. Pro Lingua is grateful for permission to continue the publication of the series.

Dedications:

> *From Rob:* This book is dedicated to the staff at RIS in Toronto.
> *From Kyoung-mi:* This book is dedicated to my family.

Acknowledgments:

Photographs:	Kum Won-sub, Rob Whyte, and Nova Corporation 250,000 Images
Sketches:	Lee Og-young
Copy editors:	Robert Bezjack and Virginia O'Brian
Clip Art:	Nova Corporation 750,000 Images

Aside from the many people who have contributed to this book working with the authors, Pro Lingua is grateful to Young-Jai Lee of Foreign Language Limited in Seoul for his editorial and cultural review of the material and his helpful suggestions.

This book was designed and set in Palatino text and Mistral display types by A. A. Burrows, following the series design by Judy Ashkenaz. He also designed the cover. It was printed and bound by Boyd Printing in Albany, New York. Palatino is an elegant modernist type face designed in 1948 by Hermann Zapf. For contrast, the titles are set in Roger Excoffon's informal script face Mistral.

Second edition, first printing 2006. 6000 copies in print.
Printed in the United States of America.

Land of the Morning Calm

Contents

CONTENTS

Shopping districts are often crowded on weekends.

Introduction

When most people are asked to name one or two Asian countries, China and Japan usually come to mind first. And why not? Both countries possess long and colorful histories, they are major players on the global political and economic stage, and each has produced a unique set of well-known cultural icons. Chinese cuisine, the Great Wall of China, and Tiananmen Square are recognizable Chinese icons. Sushi, Sony, and Toyota are globally recognized symbols of Japan. China and Japan define Asia for many Westerners.

Hidden under the China-Japan Oriental blanket is South Korea. In the West not much is known about this gem of a country except that it served as the backdrop for the popular American TV show MASH. Korea's relative obscurity is unfortunate because it compares favorably with its two Asian neighbors. It has a long, fascinating history, it has many well-preserved ancient sites and relics, and it is a thriving modern society based on a 2,500-year-old system of beliefs.

The purpose of this book is to give Westerners a brief introduction to South Korea. It doesn't try to provide colorful descriptions of all things Korean, nor does it guide tourists to the most popular attractions – a number of books already on the market do that fairly well. Instead, this book is designed for students and teachers, tourists and business travelers who want information that will make surviving, living, and working in Korea easier and more interesting.

We use the word "survive" in recognition of the fact that life in Korea is not always easy. Visitors should not expect a few weeks of rest and relaxation on balmy beaches;

1

Thailand and the Philippines are much better equipped for that kind of Asian experience. On the contrary, Korea will take you out of your comfort zone. Running headlong into Korea's often fascinating, usually bewildering, two-millennium-old culture will challenge the way you think about the world and yourself. For the adventurous, this is a place where Westerners can intermingle with a vastly different culture.

Westerners who come to Korea are sure to encounter culture shock. From the historical forces that shaped the belief system to the organization of contemporary society, every important aspect of Korea is unlike Western life. The unique and challenging quality of this country should not deter anyone from coming. After all, the hallmark of any truly memorable trip is the opportunity to experience something new and, in doing so, to learn something about oneself. Seen from this point of view, Korea can be a great trip.

Getting you ready for a fascinating adventure is what this book is about. Chapter 1 sets the stage by explaining the basic information every visitor to Korea needs to know. Banking facts, an introduction to the food, and a description of the different kinds of housing are three examples of the topics covered in this chapter.

Chapter 2 provides the reader with important country facts. One of the main themes of this book is that first-time visitors to Korea will experience culture shock, and that knowledge is one way to overcome this potentially negative experience. For this reason, Chapter 2 includes a snapshot of Korea's tumultuous 20th century. By understanding a bit about modern Korean history, it is possible to appreciate, however modestly, the why and how of modern Korean society.

Chapter 3 highlights the important aspects of Korea's customs and values. Continuing on the theme that knowledge is power, this chapter includes a brief overview of Confucius, the Chinese philosopher whose ideas have shaped Korean thinking.

A peaceful bridge located in the woods surrounding a Buddist temple.

Chapter 4 describes various forms of polite behavior. All countries have standards for good and bad manners, and Korea is no different in this regard. What sets Korea apart from the rest is that proper social etiquette entails a complex web of rituals coupled with an astute awareness of one's circumstances and the social position of other people. In most cases, visitors will not be expected to know or follow these rituals. However, foreigners who want to develop long-lasting relationships should learn and follow these codes of conduct.

Chapter 5 provides information regarding employment and immigration. Each year, thousands of foreigners come to Korea in search of work. Some leave after a short time, utterly frustrated by what appears to them to be a strange sense of right and wrong. This is unfortunate because a number of problems might have been resolved through a combination of patience and an appreciation of how Koreans see the world.

Chapter 6 provides a simple Korean pronunciation guide. Though the Korean language is complex and takes years to master, the alphabet is quite simple and can be learned in two or three hours. Knowing how to read Korean will greatly enhance the quality of one's time in this country by simplifying daily tasks. A selection of words and phrases commonly used for traveling, shopping, and eating are also included in this chapter.

Finally, a few notes about terminology. This book uses a variety of terms to describe non-Koreans. The term "Westerner" is meant to describe people from Europe, Canada, the United States, Australia, and New Zealand, regions and countries founded on the principle of liberalism or the idea that individuality should be regarded highly in society. As any visitor will discover, the concept of individualism is foreign in Korea. The term "expat" means expatriate and describes people from one country who live in another. The word "foreigner" describes people who are not from Korea.

All monetary amounts expressed in dollars refer to U.S. dollars.

For the sake of brevity, we use the words "Korea" and "Koreans" when referring to South Korea and its people. As most readers know, there are two Koreas. The other one is officially called the People's Democratic Republic of Korea. Throughout this book, we refer to it by the common name "North Korea."

1. First Steps

This section describes the basic information which foreigners need for day-to-day living in Korea. As many essential services are not readily available in English, asking a Korean friend to help is a good idea. If a friend is not available, it is acceptable to stop someone on the street and ask for assistance. Many young and middle-aged Koreans have spent several years studying English, so chances are good that you will find someone who can speak enough English to help you get what you need. Do not be shy about asking for help as most Koreans would love the opportunity to meet a foreigner, though their culture does not allow them to take the first step. Unless you are especially unlucky, the person you meet on the street will go to great lengths to help you in any way possible. The high level of kindness and sincerity exhibited by Koreans is often pleasantly surprising.

1. First Steps

1.1 Money and Banks

The Korean currency is the won. It comes in three paper denominations: 1,000 won, 5,000 won and 10,000 won. There are four coins: 10 won, 50 won, 100 won and 500 won. When carrying large amounts of cash, Koreans often use bank drafts called "supyo" which can be purchased from banks in any amount, usually from 100,000 won and up. As a general rule, it's a good idea for foreigners in Korea to avoid supyos, since store clerks sometimes refuse to accept them from foreigners

The won is a soft currency. It is strictly regulated by the government and is not widely used outside Korea. Therefore, visitors should not buy won before entering the country because the exchange rate will be lower than the market rate in Korea. Visitors leaving Korea should exchange all won at the airport prior to departure. All currency exchange services accept U.S. and Canadian dollar traveler's checks as well as Japanese yen. Many services also exchange British pounds and Euros, while the largest banks may accept other currencies. Not all banks are permitted to exchange currency. Authorized foreign exchange banks will have a "Money Exchange" sticker in the window.

Banks are open weekdays from 9:00 a.m. to 4:30 p.m. and are closed Saturdays and national holidays. ATMs (automatic teller machines) are widespread. Post offices offer some banking services such as savings accounts and ATM cash cards. When conducting bank business, or writing any person's name, red ink should never be used as only the names of the dead are written in red.

Foreigners who work legally in Korea can open savings accounts but there are no personal checking accounts. Instead of personal checks, Koreans use supyo or bank transfers to move funds to other accounts. Expats can wire money out of the country but should bring a voided check from their home bank account to an authorized foreign exchange bank in Korea because it contains the detailed information required for transfers. In order to complete a wire transfer you'll also need your passport and alien registration card. Some institutions also require a copy of your employment contract to demonstrate that you earned the money legally. Foreign exchange regulations are complex and ever-changing, so it is necessary to talk with Korean bank staff to obtain up-to-date information. If their explanations seem unreasonable, simply visit another one, since Korean bank staff do not uniformly understand or enforce regulations related to money wires or the sale of traveler's checks. For those unable or unwilling to deal with the banks, there is a black market for U.S. dollars. In busy districts, elderly women sporting large black purses and cell phones stand waiting on the street offering below-market exchange rates.

Generally speaking, the cost of living in Korea is high and in some respects compares with that in Japan. Annual inflation is between 5 and 15 percent, depending on the commodity and the source of information. Given the won's instability in light of Asia's economic crisis and a relatively high inflation rate, it is impossible in this book to estimate accurately the cost of living and traveling in Korea. Some cost data has been provided in this book, though the reader is cautioned to regard these figures as only "ballpark" estimates. For the purpose of estimating these costs in American currency, the exchange rate used for one US dollar was 1,100 KRW, the rate as of mid-2005.

1.2 Food

One of the great adventures in Korea will be the food. It is flavorful and colorful, and the entire eating style is quite different from what Westerners are used to. For the truly adventurous, this is a great place to sample tasty exotic dishes such as octopus stew, dried squid, and raw fish.

A typical breakfast, lunch, or dinner consists of a bowl of rice, soup, and several side dishes that may include vegetables or fried fish. Vegetables, especially garlic, red pepper, and soybeans, dominate the diet. There are also many noodle and seafood dishes. Koreans love to eat beef, pork, and chicken, but not to the same extent as Westerners. Strict vegetarians will need to be selective, because many vegetable dishes and soups are made from chicken, beef, or fish stock. Most people eat with a spoon and two chopsticks, though Western-style restaurants provide knives and forks.

Given the liberal use of garlic and red pepper, Korean food is typically spicy. The most popular spicy food is kimchi, Korea's national dish. Kimchi is made from salted vegetables covered with a mixture of fish oil, garlic, red pepper paste, and other spices. Cabbage, radish, and cucumber are common kimchi vegetables, but there are many others. After washing and salting, the vegetables are covered with spices and left to ferment in clay pots. The result is a delicious vegetable that can become addictive. Most foreigners either love it or hate it. Every meal including breakfast, will have at least one kimchi dish.

There are many kinds of soups and stews in the Korean diet. Three popular dishes are soybean stew, kimchi stew, and ramyon. Soybean stew has a dark, rich broth made from soybean paste, tofu, and vegetables. Kimchi stew is made from kimchi, water, and vegetables and is hot. Ramyon is an instant soup with noodles and is prepared by adding hot water. It is very spicy and makes a nice light snack.

Dried red pepper is ground and used to make red pepper powder, a staple in the spicy Korean diet.

Raw seafood is a Korean delicacy. Live fish are cut into thin slices and served on a platter along with a small bowl of hot green mustard. Other seafood, such as shrimp, are served raw without preparation. In the better restaurants, uncooked seafood will continue to twitch on the plate as it is served to customers. Some people are cautious about eating raw seafood during the summer months because high temperatures support dangerous levels of bacterial growth. Raw seafood is expensive and is an acquired taste.

For those with less exotic tastes, there are several scrumptious beef dishes. The most popular are kalbi and bulgogi, two types of meat barbecued on a small grill at the dinner table. After cooking, each person takes a piece of meat and puts it on a leaf of lettuce. Many people then add a slice of raw garlic and spicy soybean paste. Next, fold the leaf into a small bundle and pop it in your mouth. A kalbi or bulgogi dinner is an expensive but worthwhile treat for die-hard meat-eaters.

When ordering meat in a restaurant, the menu will list prices on a per serving basis, which are generally between 100 and 200 grams. Beef is generally expensive and depending on the quality and cut can range between $4 and $30 per serving. Beef from locally raised cattle, called Hanu, usually commands the highest prices, though some will argue there is virtually no difference in terms of taste or texture compared to imported products. For a more economical meal, pork is a better option with prices between $2 and $5 per serving. Samgyupsal - which means three layers - looks like Western-style bacon and consists of a thin strip of meat surrounded by fat. It's an extremely popular cut in Korea where meat-eaters enjoy eating the fat as much as the meat. For a leaner cut of meat, moksal is a superior option. It looks like a pork chop and costs about the same as samgyupsal.

Nowadays, meals in moderately priced restaurants are followed by a few pieces of fruit such as apples, pears, or persimmons, or by a drink. The typical drinks include "scorched-rice tea" (water boiled in a pot in which rice has been steamed), "scorched-barley tea," fermented rice punch, or cinnamon-flavored persimmon punch. Some Koreans will have coffee or tea. After-dinner sweets are mostly served in Western-style restaurants.

1.3 The Eating Style

The Korean style of eating meals has two interesting features. First, Koreans regularly sit on the floor at home and in restaurants, with food served on a low table. Many restaurants offer floor seating as well as tables and chairs. Second, the serving style is group-oriented. Each person has their own rice and soup bowls, while the main dishes are served in the center of the table. Everybody eats directly from these bowls and plates.

Some expats do not like the shared style of eating because of a perception that it is unsanitary, and there is one urban legend which illustrates the point. The story goes that a German and Korean were enjoying a bulgogi dinner together. To demonstrate respect, the Korean used his chopsticks to pick up a choice piece of meat from the grill and offered it to the German. The German was offended at the thought of eating meat touched by chopsticks which had been inside another person's mouth. The Korean eating style should not put off visitors as it is a great way to get to know people and will likely be one of the highlights of the trip.

1.4 Restaurants

Hotel restaurants offer some delicious but expensive meals prepared to Western standards. Most have English menus and staff members with English-language abilities. Expats hankering for a less expensive taste of home can satisfy their cravings since all cities and large towns have fast food outlets serving hamburgers, chicken, and pizza. Over the last five years there has been an explosion in the number of restaurants that serve Western-style food and beverages. Most are chain restaurants – like Outback, TGI Fridays, and Bennigans – that offer a wide array of food choices not readily available elsewhere in the country. The quality of the food has been adapted to meet the tastes of the local market, so it doesn't always meet Western standards, and the cooking methods are sometimes suspect, as in the case of one place that microwaves steaks. Despite the fact that a family outing could easily cost $100 or more, Western-style chain restaurants are extremely popular.

For everyday eating, simple Korean restaurants offer simple, economical meals. Menus are posted on the wall in Korean, so if you cannot read the menu, simply look at what other people are eating and point to the food that looks good. The server will understand what you want. A simple meal, such as kimchi stew with rice and side dishes, will generally cost about $4.00.

At the end of a meal, the waiter or waitress will bring one bill to the table, as it is customary for one person to pay. The bill is paid at the desk near the exit and cash is never left on the table. After finishing the meal, it is polite to leave immediately because customers do not relax in restaurants. To finish a conversation or enjoy an after-dinner coffee, people often go to a coffee shop or tea house.

1.5   Coffee Shops and Tea Houses

There are thousands of coffee shops located all over the country. Most shops have modern interior designs and offer snack food. After purchasing a beverage, it is acceptable to stay as long as you want. Customers are never hassled to buy something else or to leave. Tea houses are usually located off the main streets so they are some-what difficult to find, but your trouble will not go unrewarded, as this traditional cultural experience is a unique treat. Ask a Korean friend about the correct method of making and drinking tea to enjoy a surprisingly relaxing experience. The most popular tea in Korea is green tea. Koreans do not drink tea with milk or sugar.

1.6   Tipping

Tipping is rarely required in Korea. The one exception is in Western-style hotels, restaurants, bars, and nightclubs where a 10% service charge and 10% VAT (value added tax) will be added automatically to the bill. It is not necessary to tip taxi drivers. From time to time, it might be prudent to offer a small gift to someone who has provided especially good service. In these spe-cial circumstances, be assured that the gift will be received with great appreciation and will help secure future assistance.

Smoking is common among Korean men.

1.7 Drinking and Smoking

Most bars stay open until midnight or 1 a.m. during the week and 2 a.m. on weekends. If busy, the owner might close the curtains and continue serving until the place is empty. In designated tourist areas, bars may stay open all night. Alcohol can be purchased in convenience stores, department stores, and supermarkets.

Smoking is common for Korean men, and they smoke almost everywhere, but it is unusual to see women smoking in public. In recent years, an increasing number of young women have picked up the habit, though social norms require them to keep it in private areas such as coffee shops and bars. Unlike the good old days when a pack of cigarettes could be had for less than a dollar, the national government has taken steps to curb consumption by increasing tobacco taxes. Currently, the price of a 20-pack is $3.00.

1.8 Short-Term Accommodation

Visitors have three short-term accommodation options: hotels, yeogwans, and minbaks. Hotels, especially the international chains, offer comfortable rooms with standard amenities such as color TV, full bath and shower, phone, table, chairs, and a wet bar. All hotels have fax machines and will exchange US dollars and Japanese yen at below-market rates. Hotel charges can be paid in cash or by credit card. Before checking in, it is acceptable to bargain for a lower price by asking for a corporate rate or some other discount. Most people never pay the full rack rate. Room rates for international hotels are comparable to, if not higher than, those in many Western capital cities. Long-term residents who frequent hotels can combat high charges by joining the hotel's membership club. Typically, guests pay a one-time fee, which can start at $200 for a modest tourist resort hotel, and receive a booklet of coupons for free room nights, access to on-site leisure facilities, and discounted dinners. For frequent guests the cost savings can be significant.

Yeogwans are a second option and offer good value. As the Korean version of a budget motel, there are thousands of independently-owned yeogwans scattered across the country, so finding one in a good location will not be a problem. A typical yeogwan provides a small room, a color TV, and a dresser. There may or may not be a bathroom. In the cheaper establishments, there will be a common bathroom on each floor.

Guests can usually choose between a twin-mattress bed or a futon on the floor, which is the traditional Korean bed. Futons are comfortable but if you are not up for it, point to the futon and shake your head. The owner will understand that you want a Western-style bed. While creature comforts are somewhat lacking by Western standards, most yeogwans will meet the traveler's basic needs. One drawback is that yeogwans are not equipped with laundry facilities. As a result, guests must wash their clothes by hand or pay an exorbitant fee to the local laundromat operator, because coin-operated laundromats are rare in Korea. Occasionally, it may be possible to use the yeogwan owner's washing machine, but to do this you will need to be irresistibly charming and speak a little Korean.

13

Yeogwans vary enormously in terms of quality and price. Some places compare nicely with Western motels, while the bottom end can be unpleasant. Low-budget yeogwans offer cramped rooms frequented by couples who will check out after a few hours. Despite the clientele, they are safe and ideal for budget travelers or long-term residents willing to substitute savings for comfort. Depending on the quality and location, one night in a budget yeogwan typically costs $25 to $50. It may be possible to negotiate a lower rate for longer stays. Credit cards and reservations are generally not accepted. Over the past few years, a niche market has emerged for yeogwans with high-end amenities. Sometimes called boutiquetels, these places offer exciting rooms equipped with stimulating features like two-person tubs, steam showers, cozy beds, and large plasma-screen TV's. The rooms are terrific and often better than traditional hotel rooms, though there are usually zero on-site facilities. A fully equipped high-end room will generally cost between $60 and $150 per night, depending on the location and time, with higher prices on Saturday nights.

Minbaks are the third type of short-term accommodation. They might be called a lodging house or bed and breakfast, though neither term is quite correct. A minbak is a room in someone's house that is rented to travelers. Minbaks are not suitable for long-term housing but are ideal for groups traveling in the countryside.

Minbaks are in small towns conveniently near mountains, hiking trails, and Buddhist temples, but they are lean on amenities. Meals are not served and the room may consist of nothing but a bare floor, so it is a good idea to bring a sleeping bag, food, and a portable gas burner for cooking. They do not have laundry facilities, inside toilets, showers, or hot water, but that is expected, because guests pay for the proximity to the great outdoors. So, after waking up in the morning, take a deep breath of mountain air and get refreshed by washing your face in the garden with ice-cold water.

Minbaks are popular with students and summer travelers because rooms are rented on a flat-rate basis. The room charge is the same for two people or thirty, economical for large groups. Beware of minbaks occupied by students on school trips; they will party the night away with drink and merriment.

1.9 Long-Term Accommodation

Employers provide expats working in Korea with housing. Skilled professionals contracted by large corporations are housed in either a hotel or a comfortable apartment. Language teachers are provided with a lower level of comfort. A typical employer will house teachers in a shared or unshared apartment minimally furnished with a fridge, bed, and counter-top, two-burner gas range.

Renting a comfortable apartment in Korea is expensive. Typically, the employer gives the landlord a deposit called "key money." This can easily exceed $50,000 for a two-bedroom unit. Apartment leases are usually for two years. During that time the tenant is not required to pay monthly rent but does pay a monthly maintenance fee plus the cost of heat, electricity, water, and telephone. Over the past few years, a growing number of landlords have come to appreciate the value of cash flow and will rent properties for a lower deposit combined with non-refundable monthly rent. Depending on the value of the property, its location, and the current interest rate, each $5,000 to $10,000 reduction in key money will require $100 per month in rent. A third renting option is popular with single people on an extended stay. In exchange for a small deposit – perhaps $2,000 to $10,000 – tenants pay a high monthly rent that could easily range between $300 and $800 per month, or upwards of $8,000 for luxury apartments. At the end of the lease, the key money is refunded without interest.

Some teachers have a home-stay with a Korean family. The guest usually gets a separate bedroom with minimal furnishings. Home-stays provide expats with an in-depth look at Korean culture, but they are not suitable for everyone. Although the host treats the visitor as a member of the family, meals may not be included, and the visitor may be expected to take part in family activities during weekends and vacations. There may also be a curfew or strict rules about bringing friends home. The host usually gets monthly rent, but in many cases this is waived in exchange for a few English lessons. If considering a home-stay, be sure to discuss all details with the family before making a commitment. Home-stays are found through word-of-mouth and in the classified section of English newspapers.

1.10 Mass Media

The Korea Herald and *The Korea Times* are English newspapers providing limited overseas and domestic news. For better international and local news, *The International Herald Tribune,* published locally by the Joong Ahn Daily, is the best English-language newspaper in the country. It's not widely distributed and a little pricey off the newsstand, but home delivery is available in most parts of the country with substantial cost savings. Large bookstores carry several popular English-language magazines such as *Time, Newsweek,* and *The Economist* at premium prices.

There are two English-language television stations based in Korea. Arirang TV is a cable channel that carries programming about Korean culture, community events, and news. The second station is AFKN, the television and radio arm of the American military in Korea. The primary function of AFKN is to provide news and entertainment to service members stationed in Korea, so its programming is dominated by sports, late-night talk shows, and morale-boosting demonstrations of military readiness. There are two AFKN radio stations, one each on the AM and FM bands broadcasting American music, news, and talk shows. AFKN TV and radio broadcast signals are weak, so it is not possible to receive them in all areas. A cable TV subscription may provide you with AFKN television as well as CNN International and BBC World, though the hook-up fees can be mysteriously high for foreigners.

1.11 Internet Services

Over the past few years, the Internet has really taken off in Korea. Residents in large cities who want to send or receive email, or surf the Net, can get on-line at an Internet cafe. Many cafes also have computers and printers which are useful for printing resumes and cover letters. For long-term residents, an Internet connection at home is available for about $30 per month. Connection speeds vary between 24.6 K and 56.6 K. Larger Internet service providers have English-speaking customer service staff.

Although expensive, cell phones are extremely popular in Korea.

1.12 Telephones

Public pay phones use coins or plastic phone cards which can be purchased from convenience stores and newspaper stands. All pay phones can be used to make international calls. A telephone at home is easy to get and can usually be installed in one or two days. The monthly service charge is comparable to that in North America, though long-distance calls are expensive.

The international country code for calling Korea is 82. Korea is on Korean Standard Time (KST) which does not change to daylight savings time. KST is nine hours ahead of Greenwich Mean Time (GMT) and 14 hours ahead of Eastern Standard Time (EST).

Cellular phones are everywhere in Korea. From elderly grandmothers to elementary-school children, almost everyone in the country has one. When they first emerged in Korea around 1996, cell phones were given away free of charge in order to entice customers away from pagers, which were all the rage back then. Today, pagers have been effectively displaced by the most modern mobile phones on the planet. Standard features on new units include digital cameras with 2.0 megapixel images, digital file download capabilities, and speaker jacks. New cell phones can be expensive, though great deals can be had if you don't mind last year's model.

1.13 Mail and Faxes

Postal services are reasonably efficient; a first-class letter to North America takes about ten days. Care should be taken when sending valuables as they sometimes disappear in "the system." To protect your packages, insurance is available but it is expensive, while registered mail is not available for all countries. Poste restante – or general delivery – services are available free of charge at larger post offices. Central post offices offer packing services that are a treat to watch. Simply hand over your goods and in a matter of minutes, a made-to-measure cardboard box with padding is custom created. International courier packages are easy to send as there are a number of express cargo companies that offer door-to-door service and have English-speaking staff. All hotels and many small shops offer fax services, charging per page.

1.14 Transportation

The train is the best way to travel around the country. It's fast and efficient. The quickest way to travel across country is the KTX train. Depending on the time, the 450 km run between Seoul and Busan can be covered in slightly less than 3 hours with speeds that approach 300 kilometers per hour. As improvements to the high-speed track are completed, this time will be greatly reduced. KTX is expensive, but travelers on a budget can save a few bucks with a ticket for economy class, where the seating comfort is comparable to the rear section of an airplane. Travelers who require space would do well to consider upgrading to the first-class section where there's ample legroom. If you're on a budget and time is less important, there are much cheaper options on the Saemul (express train) or Mugungwha (semi-express) where travel times between Seoul and Busan stretch out to 4.5 hours.

Tickets can be purchased at train stations or at travel agencies. Buying tickets in advance is recommended for weekend travel or during national holidays. The Korean National Railway sells standing room tickets on the Saemul and Mugungwha trains, so aisles can be crowded with passengers during busy periods. Snacks and beverages are sold on the train at premium prices. There is also a dining car that sells reasonable meals at unreasonable prices, so Korean travelers often bring their own food and beverages on board.

Traveling around Korea by bus is another option. Fares are inexpensive and the bus is often the only way to access small towns or out-of-the-way sights. For short trips, the bus is satisfactory, but for long voyages, it is advisable to take the train whenever possible because seats on Korean buses are not designed to accommodate the larger Western body. Seating can be snug. In addition, the traffic situation on Korea's highways can be horrific, with delays that occasionally drag on for hours.

Domestic air travel can be expensive. Flights between major cities are much more expensive than basic train service though they are comparable to KTX first-class fares. Moreover the time saving generally associated with flying is minimized because of lengthy travel times to and from the airport. For instance, a limousine bus from Incheon International Airport (the country's main port of entry for international flights) to Seoul's downtown area will cost between $8 and $12 and could take up to 2 hours depending on traffic. If you're flying domestically, consider flights to or from Kimpo International Airport instead of Incheon because of its central location and ease of access to the downtown via the airport terminal's subway station. Kimpo used to be Seoul's principal international airport but was demoted to a regional facility after Incheon International Airport opened in 2001. Today, Kimpo handles mostly domestic flights, though there are a limited number of international flights to regional countries like Japan and China.

For those traveling within a city, buses and subways are economical. Bus and subway fare is about $1.00 with no transfers allowed. Express buses cost about $1.50 and cover the same routes as the regular ones but make fewer stops. Seoul has an extensive subway network that is ever-expanding. Busan's subway system has three modern, fast, and efficient lines, while Daegu recently opened up its first line with Line 2 under construction. Subways use a multi-zone fare system: the farther the trip, the higher the fare. Buses and subways across the country start running about 6:00 a.m. and stop around midnight. Subway maps are written in Korean and English, so finding the correct station is effortless.

Taking a cab is economical for getting around the city, but it is important to understand the taxi culture. First, there are two types of cabs: standard and deluxe. Standard cabs are small, while deluxe taxis are sleek, black, late-model cars with uniformed drivers. In most cities, a 10 to 15-minute ride in a standard cab will cost about $6, while the same ride in a deluxe taxi will be double or triple. Unless you have money to burn, avoid deluxe cabs. In small towns and villages, cab drivers will double the meter fare because they charge for a return trip even though the passenger takes a one-way trip.

Second, flagging down a taxi requires some effort. If a cab stops, tell the driver the destination. If he approves – approval is not automatic – he will gesture for you to get in the cab. It is possible that the destination will not be to his liking, and he will simply turn his head and drive away. For reasons unknown, some taxi drivers are reluctant to pick up foreigners during the evening hours. Finally, for reasons of personal safety, it is recommended that women do not travel alone at night when taking a taxi.

With the exception of people living in the downtown area of Seoul, where mass transit is usually the most efficient transport option and taxis are comparatively inexpensive, buying a car can be an extremely practical option, especially for people in provincial cities where bus service can be infrequent. Driving in Korea, however, is not for the timid and requires considerable defensive skills. Before venturing onto the road it is essential to understand three important aspects of the driving culture. First, Korean driving skills are frightening. Drivers appear to navigate their vehicles in the misguided belief that they are the only ones on the road: running red lights, left-hand turns from right-hand lanes, driving down the opposite lane towards oncoming traffic, and, of course, speeding are all part of the driving culture. In other words, every imaginable driving offense is committed on a regular basis with little or no fear of the authorities because there is virtually no traffic law enforcement, if you don't include those innocuous radar cameras commonplace on major streets and highways. The second noteworthy aspect is that your car will get banged up. Dings, dents, and scratches on the side panels and bumpers will appear on your car from to time to time regardless of the amount of care you take with your own vehicle. If you're not picky about quality, the used-car market in Korea is excellent, with roadworthy vehicles going for as little as $500. The final consideration is liability. If a foreigner is involved in a fender-bender or an incident involving an injury or fatality, they may be required to prove why they were not at fault.

A number of expats who ride motorcycles quite enjoy the bike scene in Korea, though most acknowledge that it is extremely dangerous. Korean-made bikes with 125 or 250 cc engines can be purchased in the second-hand expat market for $300 to $1,500, depending on age and condition, while the same bike from a shop could cost up to $2,500. Part of the allure of riding in Korea is the freedom: bikes purchased in the expat market often don't have plates or proper ownership papers because enforcement is negligible. On the road, motorcycles weave in and out of traffic with such verve that travel time is often half of that required by a car. A word of caution is required, however: drivers without a proper license, insurance, or plate may be subject to considerable fines if caught and could be found liable in an accident regardless of fault.

In case of a vehicular accident, there is a somewhat informal process for resolving liability and settlements. Once the police have established fault in an accident, it is customary for the parties involved to work out a compensation agreement within seven days. Claims for compensation can sometimes involve bloated medical expenses and questionable cash demands for mental anguish. There is considerable pressure on the party at fault to resolve the case quickly and informally because accidents that cannot be settled within a few days move into the legal process where much stiffer penalties, including incarceration, could be handed out. Contacting a lawyer to provide guidance in this type of situation is possible, though the retainer can be significant.

1.15 Street Addresses

Finding one's way around the city can be a challenge because of the complete absence of street signs and addresses. When describing the location of a certain place, directions are usually first based on the district name, called "dong" or "gu," and then referenced to a visible landmark such as a subway station, hotel, or well-known office building. When asking for directions, it is always a good idea to draw a map.

When speaking with someone about the mailing address of a home, there are two key words to listen for. The first is "dong" which means the apartment building number. The second is "ho" which means elevator line and room number. For instance, a large apartment complex will have many buildings each with a different number, like 111, 112, etc. Each building will typically be 2 or 3 elevator lines, each with a different number, like 1-2, or 3-4, or 5-6. So, one example of an apartment address is 111 dong, 1505 ho, which means the apartment is on 15th floor on the 5th elevator line.

1.16 Shopping

For long-term residents, daily necessities will represent the bulk of the shopping experience. An open market is the place to buy fresh and relatively inexpensive fruit and vegetables. Street vendors also sell fresh produce but at higher prices. A limited selection of food can be purchased in convenience stores, which Koreans call supermarkets, though they tend to be expensive. Shoppers should note that there is no direct sales tax in Korea: the figure on the tag is the full sales price, though it is customary to haggle for a discount in open markets and small shops.

Sidewalks in busy districts are often cluttered with street vendors selling fresh produce, chicken, and seafood.

Korean department store chains such as Hyundai or Lotte, as well as a growing number of international chains like Carrefour, Wal-Mart, and HomePlus (a joint venture between UK-based Tesco and the local conglomerate Samsung) have large grocery stores. The selection is good, and they carry imported products such as wine, fresh ground coffee, cheese, and spaghetti sauce. The main disadvantages of these retail outlets are high cost and location. Department stores tend to be located in central areas, and so getting there can take time, especially for people living outside the downtown center. For this reason, many department stores provide free shuttle bus services to and from densely populated suburban districts.

Inexpensive clothes and shoes can be had in Korea, though large sizes (e.g. 36 waist for pants, size 12 shoes, and Western-sized bras) are difficult to find. Good quality hand-made suits and shirts can be purchased from tailors at reasonable prices. The area surrounding any American army base is often a good place to start shopping because the prices are competitive and the tailor will probably speak English.

When furnishing an apartment, frugal expats rarely buy new products. Instead, they search out second-hand goods from foreigners selling their possessions before leaving the country or they go on scavenger hunts. Korean people do not like used goods, so if something has been scratched or looks old, it is put on the curb as garbage. Many a foreigner has struck gold on the street by finding tables, chairs, book cases, and TVs in good condition.

1.17 Health and Safety

The standard of professional health care in Korea is satisfactory. Though it may be a notch below the level of care enjoyed by most people in North America, it is certainly better than that found in the majority of Asian countries. Generally speaking, Korea is a healthy country, and there is no need to worry about malaria, cholera, or typhoid. Long-term residents may wish to consider purchasing private medical insurance in Korea in order to avoid costly medical expenses not covered by the national scheme. There are different options available, including some that work as a savings program. For instance, after five years of coverage, a high percentage of the total premium payment (i.e. 80-95%) is returned to the policyholder, though no interest is paid out over that period of time.

Foreigners working in Korea should ensure that their employer pays into the national medical insurance program. This is easy to verify because employees receive a medical card that must be presented during each visit to the doctor. The state-run program only covers a portion of medical costs so patients are required to pay a supplementary fee for each visit to the doctor. Simple treatments usually cost a few dollars, while hospitalization can easily require $450 or more in out-of-pocket expenses. Not all hospitals accept international private medical insurance programs, so be sure to ask before checking in.

Getting medicine is easy, as almost every neighborhood has one or two pharmacies. Many drugs requiring a prescription in Western countries can be purchased over-the-counter in Korea. For those interested in alternative medicine, ask a Korean friend to take you to a traditional Korean pharmacist.

In terms of crime, Korea is a safe country. Murder and random assaults are not common; crimes targeting foreigners are rare, though they do occur, more often than not in shady nighttime entertainment districts. The incidence of petty crime is relatively low but on the rise, though it does not approach the depths or magnitude that one might experience in less developed Asian countries. Most crimes like purse snatching or theft can often be avoided by common sense: don't leave your bag or purse unattended in public areas such as an office, library, restaurant, or bar.

1.18 Electricity

Buildings are wired for 220 volts with outlets that use 2 round prongs. Therefore, appliances and equipment from Western countries cannot be used without a power transformer. Fortunately, transformers are inexpensive to purchase. When not in use, transformers should be turned off; otherwise they continue to draw power and will run up a big electricity bill at the end of the month.

The air is polluted and wild traffic roars past Gwanghwamun, the gate to the peaceful grounds of Seoul's lovely Kyungbokgung Palace, built in 1394.

A 2000 photo by Andy Booker: www-personal.umich.edu/~arbooker

1.19 The Environment

Major cities and industrial towns suffer from levels of air pollution ranging from uncomfortable to severe. Millions of vehicles on the road, combined with municipal garbage incineration and the practice of open burning on the streets, all serve to create nasty air. Drinking tap water should be avoided due to suspicions of high metal concentrations, so most foreigners arrange for home delivery of bottled water or purchase a home water filtration system. Noise pollution is a widespread problem in downtown areas as shop owners use blaring music to draw attention to their stores.

1.20 The U.S. Military in Korea

For many years, the U.S. military in Korea maintained a force of 37,000 troops in bases scattered across the country. The long-held objective of these forces was to provide a trip-wire defense against a North Korean invasion: an attack on a small contingent would trigger a powerful American reaction. Arguing that the South Korean government is capable of assuming a larger role in self-defense, the U.S. government has taken steps to reduce the number of forces in Korea by one third. This redeployment of 12,500 troops is expected to be completed between 2006 and 2008.

For several reasons, U.S. military personnel are regarded with some hostility in Korea. Some believe that the presence of U.S. forces reduces the chances of unification between North and South Korea. Critics argue this despite North Korea's army of one million troops and its propensity for engaging in provocative activities. Opponents also point to various social problems that have resulted from the U.S. military, such as prostitution and crime. Again, this is despite the fact that these same social problems are evident in every part of the country with or without a U.S. military camp.

1.21 Pyung Conversions

Korea uses the metric system for most measurements. One exception is the measurement of area. When describing the size of apartments, office buildings, or land, Koreans use a measurement called "pyung." A comfortable apartment for a typical middle-class family of four is generally 24 to 32 pyung, or 720 to 1,130 square feet. Conversions for pyung are provided below.

Table 1	
From pyung to metric	**From pyung to Imperial**
1 pyung = 3.3 square meters	1 pyung = 35.5 square feet 1 pyung = 3.95 square yards

2. *Country Facts*

This chapter summarizes key facts about Korea and provides an overview of the country's modern political and economic history. With this knowledge, it is possible to understand in basic terms some of the unique aspects of the culture, such as the deeply held distrust of the Japanese government or the keen sense of pride that all Koreans feel.

2.1 People

As of October 2005, Korea's population was estimated by the Korea National Statistical Office to be 48.35 million. It is the twenty-sixth largest country by population. There are seven metropolitan municipalities with a population over one million, which together account for 46% of the national total. South Korea is the third most densely populated country in the world after Bangladesh and Taiwan.

- Seoul 9,895,000
- Busan 3,663,000
- Incheon 2,511,000
- Daegu 2,373,000
- Daejeon 1,442,000
- Gwangju 1,426,000
- Ulsan 1,071,000

Total Urban Population: 22,192,000

The overall population density of South Korea as of 2002 was 479 people per square kilometer, which is greater than that of China, Japan, or the U.S. The urban density is actually much higher because 70% of the land area is mountainous, and therefore largely uninhabitable. Considering these factors, South Korea's urban population density is about 1,150 people per square kilometer.

As a developing country, Koreans do not have access to a plentiful supply of public services such as swimming pools, skating rinks, or urban green space. However, the overall quality of life is good. Table 2 compares Korea with three advanced and three developing countries based on five social indicators. From the data, it could be argued that some aspects of Korea's quality of life are at least as good as, if not better than, that found in other developing countries.

Table Two
Quality of Life Indicators for Korea and Other Countries

Country	Life expectancy	People per doctor	Infant Mortality[1]	Literacy Rate	Savings as a % of GDP
Korea	72	855	8	97%	35%
China	71	1,034	31	82%	43%
Mexico	74	578	26	90%	26%
Russia	68	220	20	99%	25%
Canada	79	446	6	99%	21%
U.S.A.	77	387	8	96%	17%
Japan	80	545	4	100%	30%

(1) Infant mortality is the number of deaths under the age of one per 1,000 live births.

28

2.2 Geography and Climate

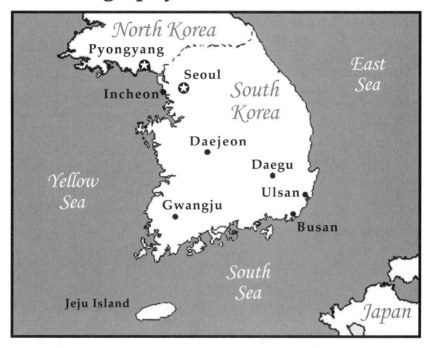

Korea is located on the southern tip of the Korean Peninsula and includes many nearby islands. The land area is approximately 100,000 square kilometers, which is about the size of the U.S. state of Indiana or the island of Newfoundland in Canada. Korea is bordered by North Korea to the north, the Yellow Sea to the west, the South Sea to the south, and the East Sea to the east. Korea and its islands lie between the 38th and 34th parallels, which is roughly the same as the states of Virginia and North Carolina.

Korea has four distinct seasons. Spring runs from March to May with temperate conditions. The summer months, June to early September, are hot and humid. Mid-July through mid-August is the hottest period with average temperatures between 25 and 30 degrees Celsius, though the high humidity can make it feel hotter. Half the country's annual rainfall occurs during the monsoon months of late June to July.

Warm days and cool nights are typical during autumn, which runs from September to November. Dry weather with a cycle of three cold days followed by four warmer ones is the norm for winter, which runs from December to March. Northeastern parts of the country receive snowfall during the winter while the southern region rarely sees snow.

2.3 Early History

History has weighed heavily upon Korea. Strategically sandwiched between three powers, Japan, China, and Russia, Korea has often served as an unwilling land bridge for powers marching into China. Despite numerous invasions and attempts to colonize the country, Korean culture remains strong and vibrant.

The corridors of power in an ancient royal palace and a pavilion in the King's Palace in Seoul.

Koreans are proud of their long and rich history. Historians have traced the ancestral roots of the Korean people back 5,000 years, while some evidence suggests the existence of tribal civilizations 30,000 years ago. Clearly, the history of Korea is far too expansive for any treatment here. However, a brief review of its modern history provides useful insights into contemporary Korean values, attitudes, and beliefs.

2.4 Japanese Colonial Rule

From 1910 to 1945, Japan colonized Korea. The colonization process started in 1904 when Japan declared war on Russia. To advance its war effort, the Japanese army occupied Korea under the guise of protecting the Korean Emperor. This was a smokescreen, as the true purpose of the occupation was the establishment of continental military bases. After handily defeating the Russians in 1905, the Japanese decided to stay and strengthen their regional dominance by taking control of Korea's foreign relations, communications, and economy. In 1910, Japan formally annexed Korea.

During the early years of colonization, Japan's focus in Korea was the efficient exploitation of its colony's economy, especially the fisheries, agriculture, manufacturing, and banking sectors. In the 1930's, Japan instituted a formal policy of cultural assimilation. Its goal was the elimination of Korean culture through programs that included the designation of Japanese as the only language of instruction in schools, the outright banning of the Korean language and the forced adoption of Japanese names. The effects of these policies linger on even today and can be noticed when meeting older Koreans who still speak Japanese and have Japanese names.

Japanese rulers in Korea encountered little organized resistance. There were periodic outbursts of guerrilla attacks, but they proved fruitless against the mighty Japanese army. The biggest protest came on March 1, 1919, with a nationwide Declaration of Independence in which 2 million people took part in peaceful marches. Caught off guard by the secretly organized protests, the Japanese leadership responded with violence. An estimated 7,000 people were killed and another 15,000 injured. Today, March 1 is a national holiday commemorating the national demand for freedom.

During the colonial period, the Japanese government sanctioned a number of atrocities. One example was the use of female prisoners as sex slaves. These women, called "comfort women," were taken to Japanese military camps around Asia and forced to provide comfort to Japanese soldiers. Women from Korea as well as other countries were taken for such purposes. At one point in time, Japanese officials downplayed their government's responsibility by suggesting that the women freely offered their services as prostitutes, though evidence given by these women suggests otherwise. The Japanese government's failure to acknowledge its past deeds and provide compensation to comfort women, as well as its perceived failure to offer an apology which satisfies the Korean concept of redemption, continue to skew formal Japanese-Korean relations.

The colonial period ended in 1945 with Japan's defeat in the Second World War. The end of the war did not, however, lead to Korea's liberation. Instead, Korea was subject to a new master: the dictates of the Cold War. The Soviet Union and U.S. agreed that both superpowers would occupy Korea, effectively dividing the country in two along the 38th parallel, with the Soviets taking the north and the U.S. controlling the south. Attempts to establish a national government failed and in 1948 two new countries were formed: the Republic of Korea (South Korea) and the People's Democratic Republic of Korea (North Korea). This set the stage for the Korean War.

2.5 The Korean War 1950-53

From 1946 to 1950, the Soviets and Chinese built a communist party and war machine in North Korea. They trained thousands of soldiers and equipped the North Korean army with guns, heavy artillery, tanks, and fighters. By June 1950, the formidable North Korean army had 150,000 to 200,000 troops. In contrast, the disorganized South Korean military consisted of fewer than 100,000 ill-equipped and poorly trained soldiers.

In June 1950, the North Korean army launched a swift attack. The goal was to create a unified communist Korea through military force. Seoul was taken in three days, and by August most of the country had been captured except for a small area around Busan, which at that time was called Pusan *(see page 86)*. A complete victory was prevented by U.S. President Truman's decision to enter the war. In September 1950, General MacArthur, commander of the United Nations troops in Korea, landed a force at Incheon, a port city just west of Seoul, and the course of the war changed abruptly. Within weeks, UN forces had retaken South Korea and were marching across the 38th parallel. Encountering little resistance from the battered North Korean army, MacArthur captured Pyongyang and was on his way to the Manchurian border.

Meanwhile, China decided that the sudden change of events was unacceptable. It responded by assembling 850,000 troops and launching a major offensive in November 1950. The enormous Chinese military pushed MacArthur back and was able to contain the UN force near the 38th parallel. For the balance of the war, the two camps engaged in a see-saw battle, as neither side was able to make a breakthrough. Fighting continued until July 27, 1953, when a cease-fire agreement was signed at Panmunjom. Technically, the two Koreas are still at war as a formal peace treaty has never been signed.

This monument stands in front of the United Nations Cemetery in Busan, commemorating the soldiers who died during the Korean War.

The war had a lasting impact on the Korean peninsula and the region as a whole. First, unification of the two Koreas seemed less likely with the entrenchment of two hostile forces on either side of the demilitarized 38th parallel. Second, political and military tension on the Korean Peninsula was heightened and remains high to this day. Third, the war spurred Japan's industrial recovery, leading to the creation of an economic superpower. Finally, the war left the Korean peninsula in a state of utter destruction, poverty, and rubble. Rebuilding would be a long and formidable project.

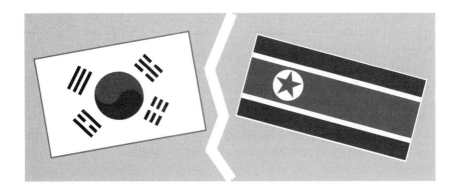

2.6 North Korea

After 1953 the truce, a stable but brutal government was established in North Korea. Kim Il-sung built a regime that was perhaps more Stalinist than Stalin himself. Kim's political ideology was largely based on a policy of "juche" which meant political, military, and economic self-reliance. After four decades in power, Kim died in 1994. His son, Kim Jung-il, took the reins of power and has continued his father's policies of isolationism and state control over society. Today, North Korea is a militarized dictatorship, and though one of the poorest countries in the world, it is suspected of manufacturing and selling advanced military weapons. According to U.S. government data, North Korea's military budget is approximately 5 billion U.S. dollars per year, or 25 percent of its gross domestic product (GDP).

Over the past few years, a deadly combination of droughts and floods has crippled North Korea's important agricultural industry. Government expenditure has been concentrated on maintaining the military. International observers believe that starvation is occurring in many parts of the country, though this cannot be verified because of the secretive nature of the North Korean government. Of the country's 24 million citizens, some estimates suggest that 5 to 10 percent of the population has starved to death. In 2000 the terrible state of the North Korean economy prompted both North and South Korea to initiate formal talks between the two former combatants. The leaders of the two countries actually met for the first time since the initial division of Korea in 1948. There was international support for "ending the war," but both North and South Korea remain deeply suspicious of each other. In 2001 Noth Korea reacted very negatively to several positions taken by the new U.S. administration, which slowed progress towards peace. Then in 2002 North Korea admitted to having a covert nuclear program. Peace initiatives foundered. Although an international coalition including China, Russia, Japan, and the U.S. have continued to try to broker a peace, as of 2005 relations between North and South Korea remain in tense and deepening stalemate. Many Koreans consider reunification a goal but not a realistic possibility. The history, culture, and economies of the two countries are very different.

2.7 The South Korean Military

Korea maintains a force of about 690,000 troops at a cost of 15 billion US dollars per year, or about 3% to 5% of the country's GDP. A conscription program requiring men to complete 26 months of duty supports the military. Typically, male students complete one or two years of college or university and then enter the military. Three years later, they return to school to finish their education. Military exemptions are a contentious issue in Korea as members of wealthy and politically connected families appear to gain a disproportionate number of exemptions for their sons.

2.8 South Korea's Economic Miracle

After the cease-fire agreement, South Korea was a razed country. There was virtually nothing left; the country was broke, and most people were fortunate to have one meal per day. In 1956, 60 percent of the national budget came from foreign aid, primarily from the U.S.

Some fifty years later, South Korea has a highly developed industrialized economy with a stable government and a literate population. It is a world leader in the manufacture of computer chips and a global player in the production of automobiles and consumer electronics. In Korea, this dramatic change from poverty to wealth is called "The Miracle on the Han," referring to the Han River which flows through Seoul.

As shown in Table 3, the economic miracle started about 1973. From 1953 to the early 1970's, growth was slow, due in part to the war reconstruction effort and the government's poor economic policies. The next two and a half decades witnessed tremendous growth as the gross national product (GNP) rocketed from $14 billion to almost $480 billion in 1996. This achievement is the Miracle on the Han.

Table 3 – South Korea GNP Growth 1953-1996						
Year	1953	1963	1973	1982	1988	1992	1996
GNP*	1	3	14	80	173	295	480
*Billion U.S. dollars						

Source: The Korean Economy, Lee Hyung-koo. Albany, State University of New York Press. 1996.

The origins of Korea's economic miracle can be traced back to President Park Jung-hee. Park came to power in a military coup in 1961 and ruled with an iron fist. In contrast to North Korea's policy of self-reliance, Park built an export-oriented economy. One of his key decisions was the re-establishment of trade relations with Japan in 1973. While pragmatic, the cultivation of economic and political ties with Japan was difficult to accept, given that the harshness of Japanese rule was still fresh in the minds of many.

Park's second key decision was economic development through "guided capitalism." The government developed economic plans that were implemented by conglomerates which supported Park's dictatorship. Conglomerates in Korea, called "chaebol," are family-owned companies involved in a diverse range of business activities. Today, Samsung, Hyundai, Daewoo, LG, and SK are the largest chaebol, with global interests in heavy industry, electronics, shipping, construction, telecommunications, and mining. Together, these five chaebol account for 45% of Korean exports.

Park's policies and personal style served as the political and economic model for Korea. Today, this model is called "crony capitalism." Under this form of capitalism, personal relationships exist between the heads of banks, conglomerate top management, politicians, and top-level bureaucrats. Government policies are decided cooperatively through informal channels, while banks extend massive loans to corporations based on personal contacts rather than an evaluation of the firm's ability to repay. In this system, bribery and corruption are widespread. Economic and political observers have pointed to this system as one of the main causes of Korea's devastating economic collapse in 1997. In December 1997, Korea is believed to have been days away from defaulting on international debt – virtual bankruptcy – until a $57 billion rescue package from the International Monetary Fund was quickly put together.

2.9 Government

Modern Korean political history is a fascinating read for those who enjoy intrigue, coups d'etat, violent street protests, government-led massacres, political assassinations, and corruption of the highest order. Just as Korea has experienced an economic miracle, it could be argued that the implementation of a presidential form of democratic government, in place only since 1992, has been equally miraculous.

Following the formal division of North and South Korea in 1948, Rhee Syng-man assumed the presidency in the south. His term was marked by a harsh authoritarianism justified under the guise of economic development and the need to suppress pro-communist forces. A fraudulent election in 1960 sparked protests resulting in the death of 142 people at the hands of the police. By then an old and frail man, Rhee stepped down in April 1960. After Rhee, there were hopes for democratic government; however, his successor lacked the necessary political skill to lead the country out of what was becoming national chaos. The economy was stumbling, student demonstrations were common, and the public did not trust the police. The social and economic conditions were ripe for a take-over.

In 1961, there was a military coup. Park Jung-hee quickly consolidated power and established a ruthless government with unlimited presidential authority. His office was fully in charge of the economy, the press, and all things related to the public domain. He also established the Korean Central Intelligence Agency (KCIA) which effectively wiped out all political opposition.

Park's justification for authoritarianism was based on the need for central management of the economy. As discussed earlier, the period under Park's dictatorship witnessed rapid economic growth along with the birth of the powerful chaebol. By the late 1970's, Korea's economy began to sputter, and as the economy fell, student protests picked up despite presidential decrees banning such activities. The end of Park's regime came on October 26, 1979, at a restaurant where he was meeting with top advisors and the KCIA chief. Kim Chae-gyu, head of the KCIA, assassinated Park and his bodyguards.

Park's death created a tremendous power vacuum because he had centralized so much control in the presidency. A general, Chun Doo-hwan, filled the void. Just as Park before him, Chun quickly consolidated power through a series of harsh measures. Universities and colleges were closed, the press was censored, and public gatherings were banned.

The harshest step came in Gwangju City. In May 1980, thousands of people took to the streets demanding freedom and democracy. President Chun's response was militaristic. By official accounts, 200 people were killed by the army and thousands were arrested. This event is called the Gwangju Massacre.

The mid-1980's was a turbulent time in Korea. Violent student clashes with riot police were a regular occurrence as was the use of tear gas. Student demands for reform took on an increasingly anti-American tone in the belief that Korea's economic and political troubles were the result of U.S. imperialism. With a new enemy at hand, the student movement swelled into a national campaign incorporating a broad range of supporters from all social and economic classes. In the face of social chaos, Chun stepped down in 1987 and was replaced by his hand-picked successor, Rho Tae-woo. Rho's appointment ignited another round of demonstrations and he was eventually forced to call an election. Perhaps this was a face-saving measure; the cameras of the world would soon be focused on Korea with the 1988 Seoul Olympics just one year away. Rho won the three-way race with 37% of the popular vote, though some commentators have suggested that there may have been voting irregularities.

Rho's presidency brought about great prosperity, particularly for himself and his closest colleagues. During his five-year term, he collected $650 million in gifts and bribes. After dividing the spoils, he left office with a personal fortune of over $220 million.

In 1992, Korea's first peaceful transition to democratic government through a fair voting system elected Kim Young-sam.

During the election campaign, Kim promised to fight corruption, but by the end of his term, his government was in complete disgrace; his son was accused of influence peddling, accepting bribes, and tax evasion. In addition, new evidence suggests that Kim Young-sam and his party accepted a $250 million gift from a single chaebol just before the election which brought him to power. Coincidentally, it was this same chaebol, called Hanbo, which later went into bankruptcy, causing an alarming chain-reaction of business failures that set off Korea's economic crisis.

In 1997, an opposition leader, Kim Dae-jung, was elected president, promising to restructure the chaebol system and to develop a positive relationship with North Korea through his "Sunshine Policy." Since Kim had been imprisoned and tortured by the government, many people expected him to make radical changes. However, his policies were more moderate than predicted and produced startling results, a meeting between Kim Dae-jung and North Korea's Kim Jung-il and other diplomatic initiatives. In acknowledgment of this historic development, Kim Dae-jung was awarded the 2000 Nobel Peace Prize. However, as Kim's term ended in October 2002, Pyongyang admitted having a secret nuclear weapons program. The luster of his legacy as a peacemaker has also been tarnished by allegations that his triumphant trip to North Korea and his meeting with the Great Leader were secured with a $400 million transfer to someone's bank account in North Korea.

In December 2002, Roh Moo-hyun of the Millenium Democratic Party was elected, after Korea's first experiment with holding primary elections. Roh pledged to revitalize communications and economic cooperation with Pyongyang and to make Korea the hub of Northeast Asian economic growth. In 2003, North and South Korea committed themselves to peaceful coexistence and to solving differences through diplomacy. Although Roh's term runs until 2008, he may not stay on for the full duration. He has hinted several times that he would like to resign or transfer presidential powers to the cabinet or possibly to the opposition. His reasons for such an unprecedented move appear to be his distaste for Korea's rough-and-tumble political culture, yet another round of highly publicized secret payoffs, and disturbing allegations of illegal wiretapping by the country's spy agency.

2.10 Education

Despite significant political and economic turmoil, Korea's education system survived and in some respects is quite admirable. The adult literacy rate is almost 100% and Korea has one of the world's most educated populations. As shown in Table 4, an estimated 19% of the population has at least one university degree, one of the highest rates in the world. Only the United States and the Netherlands have higher rates according to 1998 data from the Organization for Economic Co-operation and Development (OECD).

Table 4 – Education Attainment Rates for Selected OECD Countries (1998)	
OECD Country	*Percentage of population with a university degree*
Korea	19%
United States	26%
Netherlands	23%
Canada	17%
United Kingdom	13%
Sweden	13%

Education is revered in Korea because it decides each student's future opportunities and limitations. A degree from a top university provides the prestige necessary to enter the elite class of society. The remaining universities fall into a lower bracket and usually guarantee graduates a middle-class lifestyle and a comparable social position. Graduates from 2- or 3-year colleges and technical schools may be able to earn a middle-class income, but they are regarded with some disdain in social circles. This is due to a social prejudice against work that is dirty, dangerous, or difficult – nicknamed "3-D" work, in Korea.

The prestige and opportunities that people are afforded through higher education are based largely on the name of the school and do

High school girls walking arm-in-arm down the street. School uniforms are mandatory in most Korean middle and high schools. Boys hanging out in front of the Busan train station.

not necessarily reflect a student's scholastic achievements or skills. Indeed, student life at a Korean university is a time for fun, merriment, and participation in clubs. By Western standards, the level of academic achievement at Korean universities is low. Though it may be easy to dismiss the Korean education system, especially when compared to Western models, this conclusion would miss the mark because the overall goal of the education system is different. In some Western countries, the goal of higher education is to reduce class differences by providing students with the training and skills necessary to improve their economic situation. In Korea, the goal of higher education is to maintain the hierarchical nature of its class-conscious society.

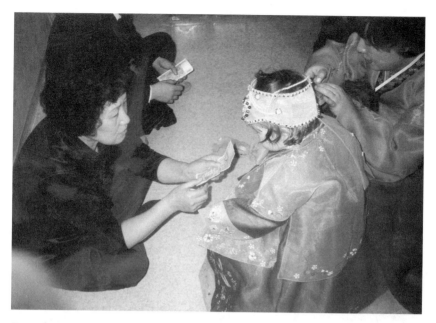

People young and old often wear colorful hanbok during Lunar New Year's and Chusok. The custom of receiving bow money has the much same sense of excitement as Christmas in Western countries.

2.11 Holidays

There are 10 to 12 national holidays each year. Some holidays are based on the Gregorian calendar, the one used in Western countries, while others follow the Oriental lunar calendar. Gregorian calendar holidays are as follows:

January 1	*New Year's Day*
March 1	*Independence Movement Day*
April 5	*Arbor Day*
May 5	*Children's Day*
June 6	*Memorial Day*
July 17	*Constitution Day*
August 15	*Liberation Day*
October 3	*National Foundation Day*
December 25	*Christmas*

Holidays based on the lunar calendar are as follows (lunar calendar dates):

January 1 *Lunar New Year's Day*
This is one of the most important events of the year. Businesses are closed for two or three days while people visit their hometowns. Many families perform ceremonies to honor their ancestors. Children bow to their parents and relatives to demonstrate love and respect. In return, children receive "bow money."

October 15 *Chusok*
Chusok is the Korean version of Thanksgiving and is the most important holiday of the year. Businesses are closed for two or three days. Many people visit family tombs to present offerings to their ancestors.

During Chusok (the Korean version of Thanksgiving) and Lunar New Year's Day, family members visit the tombs of ancestors and offer a solemn bow to pay their respects.

The dinner table is set for a Chusok celebration.
A typical Chusok dinner may include many different kinds
of rice dishes, seafood, and fresh fruit.

It is advisable to avoid traveling during Lunar New Year's and Chusok, as all modes of transportation will be booked solid. In addition, visitors to Korea would be well advised not to enter the country during these dates, to avoid the crowds and delays.

2.12 Religion

Religions are popular in Korea. According to some statistics, 40% of the population belongs to at least one mainstream religious or spiritual group. There are also a large number of "new religions" or cults which are reported to have one million followers. One example is the Unification Church founded by Reverend Sun Myong Moon, which at one time claimed to have several hundred thousand members – sometimes called Moonies – in Korea, Japan, North America, and Europe.

Statues of Buddha are common in shrines and temples in Korea. This is a very big Buddha.

In addition to the organized religions, a large segment of the population participates in shamanism. Shamanism is a belief system which holds that there are good and evil spirits in this world and that it is possible for mediums to communicate with them. Parents often consult a shaman before a child gets married to ensure that the couple is compatible. Many an engagement has been called off because of a poor report from the shaman. Parents also visit shamans just before their children write the all-important high school and university entrance exams. In rural areas, shamans may be called upon to heal people suffering from unknown ailments.

A traditional Korean dance is used to pray for good weather and a bountiful harvest.

3. Customs and Values

For the foreign resident or visitor, Korean behavior may appear incomprehensible. Bewildered visitors may ask themselves, "Why do Koreans have to act like that?" or "Why are people so rude?" Questions such as these, which implicitly try to understand one culture by comparing it to another, cannot yield any satisfactory answers. The result may be a feeling of anger and a tendency to lash out at anyone who gets in the way. This is culture shock. In order to overcome culture shock, it is necessary to be more accepting of different customs and values.

The process of accepting can be accelerated by an understanding of the major historical forces which have shaped a country's culture. To this end, the previous chapter touched upon some of the key aspects of Korea's modern political and economic history. This chapter briefly discusses the social aspects of Korean culture. To understand the organization of Korean society and the basis of its social norms, it is essential to have some understanding of Confucianism.

3.1 Confucius

Confucius was a Chinese politician, teacher, and wandering philosopher. He was born in 551 BC, died in 479 BC, and spent his life thinking about and discussing how people should behave towards one another. He was not a religious leader, nor is Confucianism a religion. Rather, his social philosophy focuses on the improvement of people and the establishment of a just society. Although 2,500 years old, his influential ideas are evident today in Korea and other Asian countries.

Confucianism is far too broad for any comprehensive treatment in this work. Instead, two of his ideas will be discussed. First is the concept "jen," an inner feeling of love for people. Jen means goodness or benevolence and encompasses those virtues which make up a moral character. For Confucius, all good leaders and harmonious societies possess this quality. Jen might be interpreted simply as the Golden Rule: do unto others as you would have them do unto you.

If jen is an inner feeling, "li" is the outer expression of this sentiment in daily life. Li is the ideal of how people should behave in society. If jen is the goal of people, li shows the way. According to Confucius, the right way to live is defined by a hierarchy of five social relationships. These relationships are: parent-child, husband-wife, older sibling-younger sibling, elder friend-younger friend, and ruler-subject.

Every relationship according to Confucius is a hierarchy. One person is the senior and the other is the junior. At work or home, the senior and junior positions are defined by one's role: the manager is above the worker, the father is above the mother, and so on. In terms of friendships, it is rare to find a relationship between two equals, as senior and junior positions are defined on the basis of age and, to some extent, gender and education background. The great emphasis placed on age in defining social positions explains why elderly people have traditionally been given a high degree of respect in Korean society.

Seniors and juniors are not simply positions in a relationship at work, at home, or in social settings. They represent two distinct sets of roles, each with a unique set of duties. A senior's duty is benevolence, while the junior has a duty of obedience. The senior should teach, while the dutiful junior plays the obedient student. If all people conformed to the duties prescribed by their roles, harmony and social order would prevail.

Harmony and social order in the Korean sense are quite different from the Western belief system. In most Western countries, these two concepts are based on a general respect for the law, hence the slogan "law and order." In contrast, harmony and social order in Korea are feelings of contentment arising from each person's conformity to the pre-determined duties of benevolence and obedience as established in the hierarchy of relationships. In the Confucian model of the perfect world, everything has a place and everything is in its place. If someone acts out of turn, there will be disharmony in the group.

3.2 Group Culture

Korean society is group oriented. Rugged individualism portrayed in Clint Eastwood or John Wayne films makes for interesting entertainment but is confounding to the Korean mindset. The concerns of the individual are always regarded as secondary to the group, and individuals who venture out on their own are rare. Evidence of group culture can be found in a variety of settings. When Koreans travel, they choose group tours. At work, co-workers often eat and socialize together. Even on blind dates, it is common for a group of six to ten people to go out together, though only two people are hoping to get hooked up.

Just as every relationship is a senior-junior hierarchy, so too are group relations. Korean society can be viewed as a package of groups organized in a series of expanding circles. At the core is the family, followed by school or work relationships. The third ring consists of other seniors and juniors. Finally, the country as a whole is one circle. Outside the last circle, and thus outside the world of Korean culture, is everything else.

3.3 Nationalism and the Concept of "We"

Koreans are very nationalistic. Proud of their homogeneous culture and long blood lines, many families maintain a family tree which dates back fifteen generations or more. This explains, in part, why sons are held in higher regard than daughters: only the son can continue the family name. Korean nationalism is openly demonstrated in a deep love for the country and the cultivation of a national sentiment called "Han." Han is the social glue which has kept the culture alive despite Korea's tumultuous history.

Korean nationalism has three other dimensions. First is the concept of "we." Stemming from the group culture mentality and rooted in the spirit of Han, Koreans do not make a distinction between "me" and "them" when discussing things Korean. There is only the concept of "we" as in "we Korean people." Thus, if a foreigner criticizes the actions of a Korean he encountered on the street, his or her Korean friends will take those comments personally, as if the foreigner had criticized them for those actions. Despite efforts to put the comments into a broader context, they will fail. In the Korean context, there is only "we."

The second dimension is a feeling of superiority. Just as Koreans view themselves as a collective "we," they see the rest of the world as a collective "them." Implicit in this distinction is another hierarchy: Koreans may see themselves in a "senior" role because they have a long lineage and a high ethical code, Confucianism, which Westerners do not share.

Xenophobia is another dimension of Korean nationalism. Korean culture has an undercurrent of suspicion regarding foreign people, ideas, and things. Perhaps this is not altogether surprising given its history of subjugation at the hands of foreigners. Notwithstanding the historical influence, the mindset of Korean culture assumes that bad things which happen in Korea are caused by outside forces.

Outward expressions of superiority and xenophobia are uncommon, however, and individual foreigners are almost never subjected to personal criticism. On the contrary, Koreans generally welcome foreigners. Most Koreans try to hide these two dimensions of their culture from foreigners, though they do surface occasionally, as witnessed by the public burning of imported products or in national campaigns targeting the "shameful" purchase of foreign luxury goods.

Foreigners who understand and respect a country's national sentiments can use this knowledge as a tool to avoid potential culture clashes and to smooth out the rough spots that naturally occur while living in a new land. When used for good, this knowledge can help visitors forge relationships that could literally last a lifetime. Failure to respect the nationalistic character of Korea's culture will only result in self-defeat.

3.4   Names and Titles

The use of names and titles in Korea reflects Confucius' influence. In any conversation, people refer to relatives, seniors, and juniors according to their title or role and not by their family or given name. A woman, for instance, will refer to her younger sister by the title, "Younger Sister." In schools, teachers will address colleagues as "Teacher Kim" rather than "Mr. Kim." In Western countries, there are a few instances of this practice, such as when we call our parents by the title "Mom" or "Dad," rather than by their given names. When addressing adult Koreans, foreigners should use the titles "Mr.," "Mrs.," and "Miss.," because there are no words in the Korean language which describe the relationship a foreigner might have with a Korean.

In Korean society, family names always come first and are usually followed by a two-syllable given name. Kim, Park, Lim, and Lee are common family names. Korean women do not change their family name after marriage. Children are given their father's family name.

3.5 Time

Different cultures have different approaches to time. Among Koreans, arriving late is not considered a serious infraction, though foreigners are expected to arrive on time. In addition, Koreans do not plan time. Meetings are usually called at the last minute and rarely start on time. Similarly, vital information required for a future task will not be provided to subordinates until the last minute, if at all. Indeed, daily decisions are managed on a "take it as it comes" basis.

Time spent at work is another example of different cultural practices. In Korea, many white-collar workers remain at their desks until late in the evening, even if there is nothing to do, because social norms dictate that employees leave after their supervisor. Thus, staff wait around until the supervisor is gone. A small number of companies have instituted a "new management" model in which workers may leave before their supervisor, though it is accepted practice to first bow and apologize for the early departure.

3.6 Personal Space

In a country with one of the world's highest urban population densities, personal space is limited. During rush hour, subways and buses are crowded. On the streets and in other public places, pedestrians routinely bump into each other without a second thought. Compounding the already tight situation, motorcyclists compete against pedestrians for space on the sidewalks.

A Korean wedding with the bride and groom wearing tradional dress, called hanbok. Notice the somber faces. According to superstition, if the bride smiles during the ceremony, the first child will be a girl.

3.7 Family Life

Traditionally, life in Korea was based on the extended family. In this structure, the eldest son had a lifelong duty to care for his parents. Thus, the eldest son, his wife, their children, and his parents and grandparents lived in the same house. The life of the eldest son was not always easy and occasionally brought about financial and mental stress. In addition, the eldest son's wife had the extra burden of caring for her in-laws. As a result, the eldest son sometimes experienced difficulty in finding a wife because many women did not want to assume the enormous domestic responsibilities which accompanied that role. Upon the death of his parents, the eldest son was usually bequeathed the greatest portion of the family's estate.

Over the past two decades, the extended family has gradually been replaced by the nuclear model: one house, two parents and children, with the son's parents and grandparents living elsewhere. Undoubtedly, this transition has been spurred on by an influx of Western values, but also by the changing economy. Increasingly, two incomes are required to pay for a home, a car, and the high cost of the children's education. As a result, many wives have had to abandon some domestic duties to earn a salary.

Whether traditional or nuclear, the Korean concept of family has a strong nurturing component. Children almost always live at home until they get married, while older siblings never fully relinquish their sense of responsibility to support  younger brothers and sisters through university and even after marriage. Important life decisions are traditionally discussed and resolved in family meetings.

While the eldest son holds an important position in the family, there is a significant gap in equality for daughters and women in general. In the past, this attitude was reflected in extreme forms of social behavior, such as abortions to terminate pregnancies after discovering that the unborn baby was a girl. Today, this practice is less common, though doctors are prohibited by law from divulging the sex of a fetus to the family after conducting an ultrasonic test.

3.8 Public Baths

Public baths are a common fixture in Korea. In the past, public baths were necessary for maintaining a clean body, as most homes did not have showers or tubs. With the development of modern bathroom facilities, the function of public baths has changed. These days, they are as much a place to relax and unwind as they are for bathing.

Upon entering a public bath, each person disrobes and takes a shower. Inside the bath house, there will be a large tub of cold water and one with hot water. Switching back and forth between the hot and cold tubs opens the skin's pores and releases deepset dirt. Outside the tub, bathers use an abrasive glove to scrub the skin. After rinsing off the dirt and dead skin in the shower, bathers jump back into the tubs. Many public baths have a sauna, sleeping area, and massage services.

3.9 Public Toilets

Most public toilets do not have toilet paper, so it is a good idea to carry a small package at all times. Used tissue should be discarded in the basket next to the toilet because the sewage systems are not designed to handle this material. In some places, both sexes use the same toilet. If the stall door is closed, it is polite to first knock. Public toilets in Korea do not always compare favorably with Western standards of cleanliness.

3.10 Singing

Koreans love to sing. At any social function, there will be singing. Sometimes people sing in order to relieve their stress. If a foreigner is welcomed to a party, he or she will invariably be asked to sing a song as a way of becoming closer to the group.

Going to a singing room is the perfect way to close a night on the town. Singing rooms are commercial establishments that rent soundproof booths equipped with electronic jukeboxes and video monitors which display the lyrics. They also have microphones, loudspeakers, tambourines, and a song catalogue. Simply enter the number of the song into the jukebox, grab the microphone, and start crooning. Most catalogues have 50 to 100 English pop songs plus a couple hundred Korean titles.

Singing rooms are an economical way to have fun and can be a real treat for those with a tolerance for ear-cracking decibel levels. They are frequented by both young and old, so if you plan on doing business, hope to establish long-term friendships, or simply want to avoid intense personal embarrassment, it is a good idea to become proficient at singing one or two songs.

Many Westerners are familiar with karaoke bars, the Japanese version of a singing room. Karaoke bars can be found in Korea but they are different from singing rooms. Korean karaoke bars have the element of singing but are upscale establishments staffed by women who, for a fee, will service every wish of the male clientele. For those with deep pockets, karaoke bars are popular places to hold evening business meetings.

3.11 Games and Leisure

Korea's professional baseball and basketball leagues are certain to be an entertaining outing for those who enjoy spectator sports. Though the caliber of play is a notch below the North American leagues, this is of no consequence because the boisterous crowds seem to have more fun than the players.

Other choices include hiking trails in the mountains, ten-pin bowling, playing games at the video arcade, and going to a video room. Video rooms are commercial establishments with small rooms equipped with a TV and VCR. Patrons can rent a movie and watch it in private. Amorous teenage couples who want to spend quiet time together regularly frequent these facilities.

Men often go to a pool hall for a few games of stick. Pool halls usually have one or two pocket ball tables, but most people play carom. Carom, or "4-ball" as it is called in Korea, is played with two white balls, two red balls and a table with no pockets. The object of the game is to score points by hitting two red balls with one cue ball in a single shot. Accurate bank shots and the ability to put the correct spin on the cue ball are required skills to win this game. 4-ball uses a simple handicap system to create a competitive game between novices and experts.

Many people practice martial arts. Japanese forms such as judo and kendo are popular, as are two Korean martial arts, taekwondo and hapkido. Taekwondo emphasizes powerful kicking and has gained an international following. It was a demonstration sport at the Barcelona Olympics and has been an official medal sport since the 2000 Games. Hapkido is a defensive fighting skill that uses kicks, strikes, and blocks.

Finally, golf has taken off in the past few years. Until recently, golf had an aura of conspicuous consumption symbolizing the excesses of the privileged class. A few companies went so far as to prohibit their managers from playing because of the poor public image it created. Everything changed in 1998 with Korean golfer Park Se-ri's success on the Ladies Professional Golf Association (LPGA) tour. Since then, golf's image in Korea has improved considerably. Many people are picking up the game, despite hefty equipment costs and green fees. Driving ranges are available in many urban areas for those who would like to practice their swing.

3.12 Alcohol and Tonics

Drinking alcohol is an important aspect of Korean culture. It stimulates male bonding, aids business deals, and plays a part in ancestral worship rituals. It is not an exaggeration to say that alcohol plays a role in daily life.

There are many different kinds of alcohol. Of course, there is beer, the quality of which may disappoint connoisseurs. Whiskey is popular and consumed in copious amounts. Business travelers would do well to bring a bottle of quality whiskey with them as it could be used to create a positive impression with their Korean counterparts. Soju, Korea's national drink, is a favorite because of its high alcohol content (about 20-25 percent) and low cost. Originally, soju was a rice wine, though mass-produced brands are now made from artificial ingredients. Other popular drinks include dong-dong ju and makoli, two rice wine beverages packing a powerful punch.

Coinciding with the popularity of alcohol, tonics or "pick-me-up" drinks are widespread. Tonics are thought to give consumers a quick burst of energy, cure hangovers, and stimulate sexual appetite. Two popular tonics are red ginseng drink and a concoction made from deer antler concentrate.

3.13 Eating Dog

Korea is a land of wonderful and exotic food. The one food which foreigners tend to avoid is dog. Dog is not part of the daily menu, but a delicacy prepared in a soup and on a platter. Dog soup is served piping hot in a bowl with vegetables. Most people add salt and red pepper to deaden the pungent aroma. Dog meat is served in thick slices and comes with a generous helping of red pepper and soybean paste. The taste and texture of dog meat is similar to a tender roast.

Some people claim that eating dog serves a medicinal purpose. During the dog days of summer, heat and humidity can quickly sap one's energy. Because dog contains a large amount of protein, the human body can recover easily from the heat. Dog is expensive and is definitely an acquired taste.

Man's best friend also plays a part in Korean traditional medicine. "Dog soju" is an herbal drink providing energy and stamina. Made from herbs and the residue of pressed dog, it has a nutty flavor and is prepared in plastic pouches. The normal prescription is three pouches per day for a month. Many people report significant health benefits ranging from increased energy and superior mental clarity to improved sexual stamina. This treatment is available from traditional doctors and is expensive.

3.14 The Arts

Those interested in folk arts will not be disappointed. Korea has a long tradition of music, painting, and dance. On the music scene, percussion groups are gaining increasing popularity. One example is "samulnori," a musical genre consisting of four musicians each playing a different kind of drum.

For art enthusiasts, a trip to a Buddhist temple will delight the senses with exquisite painting and ancient architectural styles. Most Buddhist temples are located in the countryside, so they provide the added benefit of clean air and a refreshing sense of quiet. Some cities hold traditional music and dance performances specifically targeting the foreign audience.

Fantastic art and architecture are alive in Korea's Buddhist temples. New temples, like the one at top, are often built to traditional specifications.

*Clay roofing tiles and stone walls are typical of the beautiful
architecture found in and around Korean temples.
Some walls likes these have been standing for over 500 years.*

4. Manners

Polite behavior in Korea involves a complex set of rituals for seniors and juniors. Koreans do not expect foreigners to know all the customs, and if an unintentional transgression has taken place, it will almost certainly be forgiven. However, to make a positive impression it is a good idea to learn and respect the Korean way of doing things.

4.1   Invitations

When going out with Korean friends or business associates, it is important to be mindful of who makes the invitation. The person who issues the invitation customarily pays. If you would like to go out with friends but do not have enough money to cover the cost for everybody, it is acceptable to suggest "Dutch pay" before heading out.

At first glance, the custom of one person paying might seem burdensome. However, Korean culture has a way of ensuring equity. If one person pays now, it is expected that the treat will be reciprocated in the near future. Another form of built-in equity is that if one person pays for dinner, the cost of the next stop, say a bar or a movie, will be paid by a different person.

Occasionally, a Korean friend will decline an invitation. Although the friend may truly want to go out, it is considered polite to decline an offer two times. If the invitation is extended a third time, it might be accepted. If a friend turns down your offer a third time, it is because they really do not want to go out with you.

4.2 Bowing and Handshaking

It is usually polite to bow when greeting someone. Depending on the other person's social position relative to yours and the circumstances, the style of the bow will vary. The general rule is to bend at the waist keeping the hands to the sides.

Bowing deeply to a 45-degree angle shows great respect. This deep bow is reserved for formal occasions when greeting someone of importance, such as a distinguished elderly person or company president. During less formal occasions, bowing to a 25-degree angle is appropriate, as would be the case when greeting a senior or a high-level manager in a business meeting. For everyday situations or when greeting an equal, a 10-degree bow or even a simple nod of the head is sufficient.

There is one final bow that is reserved for solemn occasions. This bow requires people to first kneel down on the floor and sit on the folded legs. Next, bend at the waist and bow down so that the forehead almost touches the floor. Place the hands together in front of your body with both palms on the floor. Finally, the forehead should rest on top of the hands. Hold the position for four or five seconds and then get up. This bow shows the greatest respect and is given to parents, grandparents, and in-laws during Chusok and Lunar New Year's as well as at ancestral remembrance ceremonies.

A polite handshake to show respect with the left hand placed over the right chest, a slight bow, and no eye contact.

Handshaking also requires an awareness of the circumstances. During formal occasions or to show deep respect, the customary handshake requires men to extend the right hand as people do in the West. At the same time, your left arm crosses your chest with the left hand placed on the right breast. Finally, bow to 25 degrees and avoid eye contact. This handshake is reserved exclusively for men. If a man is in a business meeting and would like to shake hands with a woman who is roughly the same age, it would be polite to use the standard Western handshake combined with a slight bow. If a man is greeting an older Korean woman, it would not be appropriate to shake hands. Instead, a 10 or 25-degree bow would be polite. Generally, women do not shake hands with other women.

4.3 Displays of Emotion

Koreans generally maintain a reserved appearance in public. Physical expressions of displeasure or satisfaction through frowns or smiles are not customary. However, this can change after two people become acquainted, at which point Koreans love to laugh and smile. Koreans are also uncomfortable showing their emotions towards members of the opposite sex in public. As a result, older men and women who love each other rarely hold hands in public, and couples of any age never kiss in a public place.

Two boys posing for the camera. Physical signs of affection in public are common between members of the same sex.

In contrast, affection is often displayed between members of the same sex. It is common, for example, to see boys holding hands while walking down the street or girls walking arm-in-arm. In business circles, men who have a close relationship will often hold hands momentarily after greeting each other. This behavior is not a sign of homosexuality but a simple expression of the sentiment, "I like you."

The attitude toward physical displays of affection is rooted in a concern for other people. A couple may want to kiss in a public place but will not, in the belief that it may cause other people discomfort. The same logic applies to situations that generate feelings of anger. Anger should never be displayed in public or directed at anyone. Although bursts of outrage do occur frequently, they are regarded as impolite and characteristic of a lower-class of people. Foreigners working in Korea should bear this in mind; it is unacceptable to lose control over one's emotions in front of another person. These types of inappropriate actions will result in the loss of any goodwill that may have been established up to that point.

4.4   Eye Contact

Koreans rarely make eye contact with strangers in public. Where a relationship already exists, rules for eye contact in formal settings follow the senior-junior hierarchy. During a conversation, the junior should not look the senior in the eye as this would demonstrate a disrespectful and rebellious manner. The senior may look juniors in the eye, though they may break contact when discussing serious issues. Most people understand that Westerners make eye contact during a conversation, and it will be accepted, though it would be a good idea to break contact frequently in order to avoid creating an uncomfortable situation.

Like most aspects of Korean social etiquette, the accepted norms of eye contact do not apply when looking at foreigners. Koreans, especially those outside Seoul, may stare at foreigners with an unsettling level of intensity. Though expats may regard this behavior as rude, that is usually not the intent. Often, Koreans stare at foreigners because they are curious.

4.5 Shoes

Minding your shoe manners is essential. The simple rule is as follows: if people sit on the floor, remove your shoes before entering. So, the shoes come off when entering someone's house and restaurants where people eat while sitting on the floor. When in doubt about what to do, look around for other shoes. After taking off your shoes, you will probably be given a pair of slippers to wear.

4.6 Dress

Koreans form judgments about people by their appearance and not by their abilities. Thus, if you want to be treated with a certain level of respect, you must dress the part. If you want the respect that goes with a high social position, such as a university professor, a suit and tie is mandatory. Business people should wear conservative suits and ensure that their shoes are polished. Regardless of accreditations, experience, or abilities, a teacher or businessperson wearing jeans and a sport jacket will create a dismissive attitude. Finally, shorts are acceptable for leisure activities during the summer but should never be worn by men during work hours or at work-related events.

4.7 Drinking Customs

Drinking has a unique set of rituals. An individual, for instance, should never pour their own drink and should wait for someone else to pour. If your glass is empty and you want a refill, it is a good idea to make a joke such as by asking, "What time is it?" or "Who killed President Park?" (referring to the assassination of President Park in 1979). Questions like these provide the group with a humorous hint that you are ready for another. A glass will not be refilled until it is empty, so people who want to stop drinking leave a small amount of beverage in the glass. When pouring a drink, the polite person is aware of who holds the senior and junior positions. Seniors pour with one hand on the bottle while the well-mannered junior uses two hands. The same rule applies when receiving a drink: seniors put one hand on the glass and juniors use two hands.

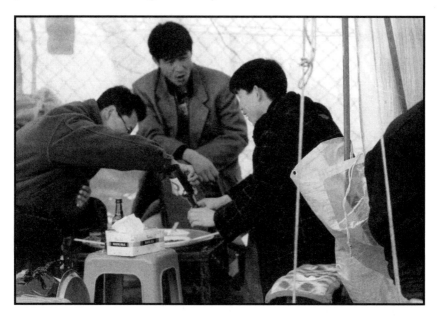

Having a drink in a soju tent. Notice that the man pouring has one hand on the bottle with the other on his chest, while the man receiving the drink has two hands on his glass. These actions demonstrate good manners.

A junior will demonstrate bad manners and remarkably poor judgment if they decline an invitation from a senior to drink. This ill-advised action can have serious consequences in business circles. In contrast, men who can consume large quantities of alcohol, and hold it, will be held in high regard. As a result, Korean men routinely quiz others about their drinking ability. To avoid embarrassment, the standard answer is two bottles of soju.

Foreign women who are able to consume large quantities of alcohol will amaze their Korean female friends and confound the men. Korean men do not generally drink socially. The idea of having one or two bottles of beer for socializing is quite foreign. However, if a Korean friend or business associate invites you out for "a drink," you should expect that the group will enjoy more than one drink.

While enjoying the company of friends or colleagues in a bar, Koreans love to munch on side dishes. In some establishments, patrons are required to order at least one side dish if they want to drink. There are many different kinds of side dishes, three favorites being french fries, dried squid, and fruit platters. Side dishes are usually expensive.

Groups will often visit three establishments while spending a night on the town. One reason for moving is to create a lively mood especially if the last place was becoming dull. Another is to give everyone a convenient opportunity to go home as it is impolite to get up from the table and leave. A third reason is to spread the financial burden because a different person will pay at each establishment.

4.8   Eating Customs

Koreans are ravenous eaters and eat with gusto. With shoulders hunched forward, Korean people do not waste precious time chatting over dinner: meals are a time for eating, not talking. To show their enjoyment of food, Koreans make various sounds. For example, the lips and tongue make a loud smacking noise while chewing and many people exhale deeply with a loud "ahhh" to show a general sense of pleasure. While eating noodles, drinking soup, or hot coffee, it is customary to slurp loudly. After taking a sip of whiskey or soju, it is common to make a loud "krrr" sound in the back of the throat. Burping in public is not polite.

These girls have stopped to buy a snack from a street vendor. They are enjoying a popular street food called ho duct,which vaguely resembles a flat donut. It is often sold in winter, fried in butter on a hot grill. The inside contains a tasty mixture of brown sugar and crushed peanuts.

Although Korea's eating customs may appear somewhat boorish to westerners, it is important to understand the context of eating. First, Korean food is spicy and often served at high temperatures. Thus, lip smacking and slurping are required gestures to cool down the food. Second, the Korean War has had a direct impact on the eating style. During and after the war, millions of people endured intense hunger, so when food was available it was consumed wholeheartedly without regard for social graces. Eating quickly was a practical skill to avoid hunger.

*Koreans enjoy eating fast food. Here two boys have ordered
hot food from a street vendor.
Sometimes fast food is eaten with the fingers,
sometimes with chopsticks.*

4.9   Gift-Giving and Thank You's

The giving of gifts to show appreciation is customary. If someone goes out of their way to help, there is an unspoken understanding that the favor will be returned. The cost of the gift is not important but the demonstration of a kind heart is critical.

When invited to someone's house for dinner, it is appropriate to bring a bag of fruit, some fruit juice, or a few cans of tuna. For birthday or thank you gifts, hand soap, underwear, and socks are good ideas. Laundry detergent is a common gift for house warming parties. If you want to give money, as would be the case at a wedding, it is polite to first put the money in an envelope. Handing over cash in any situation is bad form.

4.10 Humor

Korean culture has a unique style of humor. Sarcasm and witty put-downs will likely be taken as an insult. Instead, Korean humor uses exaggerated compliments such as, "You look more beautiful than Princess Diana," or "Do you think I look like a supermodel?" When someone makes a bad joke, it is common to say, "I feel chilly," or "That joke was cold." Koreans also enjoy slapstick comedy along the lines of Jim Carrey.

4.11 Silence

In social settings, Koreans feel awkward if there is a period of silence. In the spirit of Confucius' jen, silence shows a lack of attentiveness toward others. Consequently, most people try to ensure that the entire time is filled with talk. Of course, most cultures enjoy upbeat, light-hearted moments. What is unique about Korea is the heightened sensitivity to changes in the group's mood: when the mood turns sour, everybody feels it.

There are times, however, when silence should be created intentionally. If someone asks a highly personal question and the respondent does not wish to reply, they may fall silent as a quiet sign of displeasure or annoyance. Another example is during a business meeting when important decisions need to be made. In these situations, it may be appropriate to use a moment of silence to demonstrate a posture of sober, second thought.

Retired seniors often rest in public places to pass the time.

4.12 Business Cards

When conducting business, the first important step is to hand out business cards which identify your company, name, and job title. A name without a title will seem odd to Koreans and they may have difficulty establishing a rapport. If you do not have a title, make one up. Though it is not necessary, business people can create a favorable impression by printing cards with English on one side and Korean on the other. For obvious reasons, handing out cards with Japanese characters would demonstrate poor judgment.

When exchanging business cards, it is customary to spend a few seconds examining each card you receive to demonstrate an interest in the other person. The use of two hands when giving or receiving business cards, important documents, or gifts also shows respect for the other person.

5. Employment and Immigration

Each year, thousands of people come to Korea in search of employment as language teachers. Regulations governing this activity are ambiguous, ever-changing, and too numerous to document here. This chapter highlights only a sampling of the information required for a successful journey. Anyone interested in coming to Korea for employment should contact the Korean Embassy or a consulate in their home country in order to obtain complete information. There are also numerous Internet web sites providing a wealth of information about teaching in Korea.

5.1 Teaching English as a Foreign Language

A certain type of personality is required to have a positive teaching experience in Korea. For those who want "to find themselves," Korea is not the right place. If you are looking for that kind of Asian experience, try Thailand or the Philippines. Overly shy or aggressive characters will have difficulty adapting, because survival in Korea requires a balance between knowing when to accept things as they are and when to push. Expats who have had a positive experience are able to improvise in any situation.

A four-year Bachelor of Arts in something or other is the basic employment requirement, though better jobs can be had with a Master's degree. Teaching experience is not required at all. A number of universities seek out teachers with a Master's degree in English or Linguistics, though some people with professional qualifications do not work in Korea because better wages, superior living conditions, and a management style which supports and rewards professional development are available in other countries.

Prospective candidates should know that Korean hiring practices are discriminatory. Koreans prefer thin, white, attractive people in the 24-to-39 age bracket. Older women usually have no problem finding work, because female teachers are in demand, owing to the under-representation of foreign women in Korea. Older men may have trouble unless they graduated from a prestigious university or possess an outstanding resume. Finally, because of the strong preference for Canadian and American accents, teachers from other English-speaking countries may encounter some resistance.

The glory days of flying into Korea and picking up fast work as an English instructor seem to have all but vanished. Employment is still readily available, but in recent years the number of bureaucratic obstacles has increased. Paperwork requirements are forever changing, but a well-prepared traveler hoping to land the best possible employment position will come to Korea with a packet of important documents. These include an original university diploma, at least two letters of recommendation, and several original copies of a police check from your local police department indicating no criminal record. Korean schools are increasingly aware of the problems caused by teachers working with fraudulent degrees, and as a result document scrutiny is now on the radarscope of Immigration authorities. Past attempts to combat document fraud by requiring diploma certification at a Korean consulate abroad seems to have failed, so teachers are now required to produce sealed university transcripts (in other words, transcripts in an unopened envelope bearing the university stamp on the back). For this reason, the well-prepared job hunter would be well advised to bring several sealed transcripts in order to avoid the hassle and cost of ordering these documents from Korea.

5.2 Opportunities for Teachers

There are four main areas of employment: hagwans, the public school system, universities, and private corporations. Hagwans, the most popular places for first-time teachers, are privately-run language schools that employ foreigners as conversation instructors. Most teachers work a six-hour split-shift per day, usually three hours in the morning and three at night, five days per week. Hagwans sometimes require teachers to work a half-day on Saturdays.

Hagwan jobs have a number of disadvantages. First, vacations are short, averaging three days per year plus 10-12 national holidays. Another drawback is the low pay. Finally, a number of foreigners have experienced problems with hagwan managers ranging from the difficult to the bizarre. Before accepting an employment contract, do your homework: surf the Internet for information about the employer and try to contact current employees and ask about their experiences.

After learning the ins and outs of life in Korea, many teachers try to move up to a better job. One option is teaching at a middle school, high school, or two-year college. Expect a "9-5" job with 20-25 contact hours per week. The salary is a step up from hagwans, and the annual paid vacation ranges between two weeks and four months.

Universities are the best places to work. The average teaching load is 14-20 contact hours per week with occasional mandatory overtime. For people with a Master's degree, the pay is near the top end of the scale and many institutions provide instructors with offices, computers, and Internet access. Better universities provide four months paid vacation per year, while others have scaled it down to four weeks. A few universities provide an unshared apartment, which is a substantial benefit.

There are two types of universities in Korea. National universities, or state-financed schools, are generally more prestigious, though the pay for English language instructors is often lower than what can be had at a private post-secondary institution. The same pay discrepancy does not, however, apply to foreign instructors hired to teach content-based classes in English. There is a growing demand for professional foreign instructors – mostly but not exclusively in national universities – with sought-after specializations that cover a wide range of fields, from science to literature. Qualifications for these positions usually begin with a Master's degree and a research or publication background, though a PhD is often required.

For English language teachers, the monthly salary is usually higher at a private university, but instructors are often expected to carry a heavier class load. In addition, the sharp decline in student enrollment that has been taking place over the past few years, a trend that is expected to continue for quite some time, is driving private universities to secure alternate revenue streams. In a great many cases, these schools are opening their own private language academies and are requiring their foreign university teachers to provide the labor input. As a result, foreign university instructors are increasingly required to teach adults in the early morning and/or children in the late afternoons with overtime rates of pay that range between poor and downright awful. In light of this trend that seeks to maximize the profit potential of foreign teachers, English language instructors at private universities should expect something in the range of 16-22 contact hours per week plus 4-6 hours of office hours.

There are a limited number of teaching positions at large corporations. These jobs tend to be competitive with universities in terms of pay, housing, and bonuses, though the workday can be long. Expect to start at 7 a.m. and then to teach for one hour at a time, here and there throughout the day. One benefit is that teachers may have free access to the company cafeteria and exercise facilities.

5.3 Other Employment Opportunities

There are a limited number of non-teaching employment opportunities for those with specialized skills and experience. Examples include working as writers or editors for newspapers and other publications. There are also opportunities to work for television networks as writers, actors, and on-air personalities. Lawyers can work in Korea as legal consultants, although they cannot practice law. Rarely advertised, non-teaching positions are usually found through word-of-mouth and are located mostly in Seoul.

5.4 Employment Visas

The best way to get a teaching job is to come to Korea on a tourist visa and look around. This way, you can meet potential employers and talk to other teachers. Once you find a suitable employer and accept a job offer, fly to Japan, stay one night, and get a work visa the next day. The major drawback is that you have to pay for the flight to Korea as well as all expenses while job hunting. The other option is to find a job on the Internet or through a recruiting agency and obtain a visa before coming. The main advantage of this approach is that the airfare to Korea will be paid by the employer, while the downside is that you will not have had a chance to preview the school or manager. Prospective teachers should avoid all recruiting agencies which require job hunters to pay a fee. Teachers do not need to pay for this service, because the recruiter receives a commission from the employer. In addition, many jobs can be found on the World Wide Web without a placement agency. A great place to start job hunting on the internet is "Dave's ESL Cafe."

Korea's work permit system severely restricts freedom of employment. An employment visa allows a foreigner to work at one institution for a fixed period of time. Visas can be renewed easily for those re-signing contracts at the same place of employment, but it is difficult to change jobs before the contract is over. To do this, a teacher must obtain a "letter of release" from the current employer, which is a feat of Herculean proportions. If by chance a letter is obtained, the teacher must leave the country in order to get a new work visa and, for most people, that means another overnight trip to Japan.

A number of foreigners supplement their income by teaching individuals on a part-time basis. These jobs are called "privates" and usually involve teaching children, housewives, or business people in their homes or offices. Though illegal, teaching privates is widespread, because the income can be substantial while the chances of being caught are slim. Foreigners picked up by the Immigration Department for teaching illegally should expect a hefty fine and possible deportation.

For people who want to explore other parts of Asia while working in Korea, it is necessary to obtain a multiple-entry visa. This is another stamp in the passport that allows you to come and go from Korea as you please. Multiple-entry visas are available for a fee at the local immigration office.

6. The Korean Language

Korean is reputed to be one of the most difficult languages to learn and can take years to master. The alphabet, however, is straightforward and can be memorized in a few hours. Learning how to read and pronounce basic sounds will greatly enhance the quality of your time in Korea by simplifying everyday tasks such as taking a bus or getting a meal in a restaurant.

6.1   Basic Information

The Korean language is called Hangul. It is classified as part of the Ural-Altaic family, which includes Mongolian, Finnish, and Turkish. Hangul is not directly related to Chinese or Japanese, though the grammatical structure is similar to Japanese. Until the mid-1400s, all documents in Korea were written in Chinese because there was no Korean script, there was only a spoken Korean language. In 1443, King Sejong assembled a court to develop a written language which was eventually called Hangul. Today, the written language continues to use about 1,800 Chinese characters, called hanja, for ideas which cannot be expressed easily in Hangul. The Korean language is read in rows from left to right, though it was traditionally read in columns from right to left.

Reflecting the culture's acute awareness of social positions, the spoken language is honorific. That is to say, the language contains many degrees of formality which are used to acknowledge the other person's position. Although Koreans do not explicitly classify degrees of polite speech, it is possible to see three or four levels. This classification does not apply in every situation because politeness is contextual. As a general rule, the forms work as follows.

The highest level of polite speech is used when juniors speak to distinguished elderly people or those holding powerful positions, such as company presidents or politicians. The second level is a general polite form which is used when speaking to seniors or colleagues of the same age in formal and informal situations.

When speaking to a younger adult, a third form is used which implicitly recognizes the senior's position over the junior. This form of speech is not taken as an insult but is viewed as an objective recognition of who holds the top and bottom positions. Finally, adults use a low form when speaking to children. Children also use this form when speaking to each other.

An example of the four degrees of polite speech can be shown with the verb "to go," which is "ga" in Korean. First, when speaking to a distinguished senior, people say "gasipsio," which is the highest form of politeness. Second, the general form of politeness is "gasaeyo." Third, a senior may use "gaja" when speaking to an adult junior. Finally, "gara" is used when addressing children.

Another example of the complex nature of spoken politeness is evident with the simple word "hello." When greeting a distinguished senior, the speaker should say "Anyong hasimnika?" In less formal situations or when meeting equals or adult juniors, it is polite to say, "Anyong hasaeyo?" Literally translated, these questions mean, "Are you peaceful?" The correct response would normally be, "Nae," a simple "Yes." When adults meet a child, they will say "Anyong?"

6.2 Pronunciation Guide

Hangul is written in blocks of syllables consisting mostly of straight lines and circles. The physical shape of Hangul differs from the artful and often complex appearance of Chinese or Japanese characters. The Chinese language, for example, uses ideograms, or pictures, to express ideas rather than sounds. In contrast, each Hangul syllable represents a separate sound, so that learning how to pronounce words is relatively simple, though the meaning of the words may be unknown.

The modern Korean alphabet has 40 characters: 21 vowels and 19 consonants. The following guide shows the 12 vowels and 14 consonants which are used most often along with their equivalent sounds in the English language.

Main Vowels

ㅏ	ㅑ	ㅓ	ㅕ	ㅗ	ㅛ
"ah"	"yah"	"eo"	"yeo"	"o"	"yo"
f<u>a</u>ther	<u>ya</u>cht	s<u>o</u>me	<u>yu</u>mmy	g<u>o</u>	<u>yo</u>lk

ㅜ	ㅠ	ㅡ	ㅣ	ㅔ	ㅐ
"oo"	"yoo"	"u"	"ee"	"ae"	"a"
m<u>oo</u>n	<u>you</u>	p<u>u</u>ll	m<u>e</u>	g<u>e</u>t	b<u>a</u>t

Main Consonants

ㄱ	ㄴ	ㄷ	ㄹ	ㅁ	ㅂ	ㅅ
"g"	"n"	"d"	"l"	"m"	"b"	"s"
<u>g</u>od	<u>n</u>od	<u>d</u>one	<u>l</u>ong	<u>m</u>ud	<u>b</u>ad	<u>s</u>ing

ㅇ	ㅈ	ㅊ	ㅋ	ㅌ	ㅍ	ㅎ
"ø/ng"	"j"	"ch"	"kh"	"t"	"p"	"h"
ri<u>ng</u>	<u>j</u>ar	<u>ch</u>ar	<u>c</u>ar	<u>t</u>ar	<u>p</u>ar	<u>h</u>eart

A written syllable never begins with a vowel. In cases where a vowel is the first sound, a silent placeholder is used as the initial character. The placeholder is the same character as that used for the "ng" sound which sometimes appears at the end of syllables.

The following chart can be used as a drill to practice the most common groupings of vowels and consonants. In the far-left column of the drill chart, a placeholder is used because the first sounds are vowels. In the far-right column, the first character is also a placeholder while the same character appears at the bottom to make an "ng" sound.

아 가 카 나 다 타 라 마 바 파 사 자 차 하 앙

야 갸 캬 냐 댜 탸 랴 먀 뱌 퍄 샤 쟈 챠 햐 양

어 거 커 너 더 터 러 머 버 퍼 서 저 처 허 엉

여 겨 켜 녀 뎌 텨 려 며 벼 펴 셔 져 쳐 혀 영

오 고 코 노 도 토 로 모 보 포 소 조 초 호 옹

요 교 쿄 뇨 됴 툐 료 묘 뵤 표 쇼 죠 쵸 효 용

우 구 쿠 누 두 투 루 무 부 푸 수 주 추 후 웅

유 규 큐 뉴 듀 튜 류 뮤 뷰 퓨 슈 쥬 츄 휴 융

으 그 크 느 드 트 르 므 브 프 스 즈 츠 흐 응

이 기 키 니 디 티 리 미 비 피 시 지 치 히 잉

에 게 케 네 데 테 레 메 베 페 세 제 체 헤 엥

애 개 캐 내 대 태 래 매 배 패 새 재 채 해 앵

6.3   Substitution Sounds

Although the Korean and English languages share many of the same basic sounds, there are a few differences. For example, the Korean language does not have an /r/ so the closest sound is substituted, which happens to be /l/. When Koreans first learn to speak English, they often mispronounce some sounds, occasionally leading to an interesting misunderstanding. For example, a Korean might want to say, "Let's eat rice," but it will sound like, "Let's eat lice."

The following shows the English sounds which the Korean language does not have and the substitutes typically used in spoken Korean.

/r/ is replaced by /l/ (rice – lice)   /er/ is replaced by /a/ (meter - meta)

/f/ is replaced by /p/ (face - pace)   /v/ is replaced by /b/ (very - berry)

/z/ is replaced by /j/or/ch/   /th/ is replaced by /s/ (think - sink)
            (zoo - jew or chew)

6.4   Adopting New Words

The Korean language adopts foreign words or new technical expressions in one of two ways. The most common method is to break new words into phonetic parts and then translate them into Korean. Two examples are "computer" which is pronounced in Korean as "komputa" and "pizza" which is pronounced as "picha." Words that come from other languages are generally translated into Korean using the native pronunciation. For example, the French word "Paris" is pronounced as "Pali," not "Palis."

The second method of adaptation is to invent new words by borrowing terms, primarily from English and, to a lesser degree, Japanese. In Korea, this is called "Konglish," a combination of Korean and English. Konglish exists by taking an English word, or parts of an English word, and giving it an entirely new meaning, one which can be quite different from the original English usage. One example is the Konglish word "meeting." In English, this word can refer to a business meeting but in Korea it means a blind date. Other Konglish terms include: hand phone – a cell phone; one piece – a woman's dress; Y shirt – a man's dress shirt; open car – a convertible.

6.5   Regional Dialects

There is no regional variation in the written language, but speech is a different matter. Most people accept that Seoul residents speak standard Korean, which is spoken softly without strong intonational shifts. Outside Seoul, regional dialects are so distinct, it is possible to identify a person's home province by the sound of their words. A similar situation exists in North America when comparing accents from Newfoundland to Ontario or Arkansas to New York.

In Seoul, the standard pronunciation of "thank you" is "gomap sumnida." Residents of Busan are easy to identify because their tone is harsh and words end with a "day" sound rather than the standard "da." In the Daejeon area, words ending in "da" are pronounced as "die." Residents of Jeju Island, a fishing and resort island off the coast of Busan, speak with a dialect so strong it could almost be classified as a different language. Foreigners who learn to speak a regional dialect are sure to entertain their Korean friends from other regions. Imagine a Korean visiting your home speaking in a heavy New York or Texas accent.

Finally, Hangul in North Korea represents an example of a language in isolation. Reflecting the closed nature of its society and government, North Korean Hangul has to some extent remained static. Both the written and spoken forms use "old fashioned" words, some dating back to the 15th century, long abandoned in the south. In speech, North Korea's capital city sets the standard for pronunciation. Residents of Pyongyang speak with an intonation that produces harsh sounds in contrast to the flat, soft tone found in Seoul.

The written form also differs, as the north continues to use several letters that were dropped long ago from the South Korean version of the alphabet. Lastly, while South Koreans adopt new words primarily from the English language, the North's version of Hangul at one time developed new words borrowed from former communist countries in Eastern Europe. Given these differences, South Koreans experience some difficulty in understanding what their northern counterparts are saying.

The Romanization of Korean sounds provided below reflects changes adopted by the Korean government in 2000. Prior to that time, the government used the McCune-Reischauer system, a method of representing Korean sounds with Latin characters that was developed in 1937 by two graduate students. Although the new system seems more user friendly, it has yet to be fully implemented across the country. As a result, travelers will often see one city name on different road signs with two or three different spellings, for instance, Pusan and Busan.

6.6   Important Words and Phrases

This section presents a few simple yet important phrases that will help visitors with daily activities.

Hello (formal) Annyeong hasimnikka? 안 녕 하 십 니 까?

(general).. Annyeong hasaeyo? 안 녕 하 세 요?

(low form) .... Annyeong? 안 녕

Thank you .... gomap sumnida 고 맙 습 니 다

.... gamsa hamnida 감 사 합 니 다

I'm sorry .... mian hamnida 미 안 합 니 다

No .... aniyo 아 니 오

Yes ....nae 네

Please .... juseyo 주 세 요

Here .... yeogi 여 기

There .... jeogi 저 기

6.7 Counting Money

Counting money is relatively simple because only a few root words need to be memorized. The remaining terms are constructed by combining different root words.

zero .... gong	공	seven .... chil	칠
one il	일	eight .... pal	팔
two............. ee	이	nine...................... gu	구
three .... sam	삼	ten .... sib	십
four .... sa	사	one hundred .. baek	백
five .... oh	오	thousand .... cheon	천
six .... yuk	육	ten thousand ... man	만

From these words, other numbers can be formed.

11 .... sib il	십 일	50 .... o sib	오 십
12 .... sib i	십 이	55 .... o sib o	오 십 오
19 .... sib gu	십 구	101 .... baek il	백 일
20 .... i sib	이 십	200 .... i baek	이 백
25 .... i sib o	이 십 오	7,000 ..chil cheon	칠 천

When pronouncing large numbers, 10,000 is used as the baseline. For example, 100,000 is pronounced as "10 ten-thousand."

100,000 .... sib man	십 만
101,000 .... sib man il cheon	십 만 일 천
450,000 .... sa sib o man	사 십 오 만
777,000 .... chil sib chil man chil cheon	칠 십 칠 만 칠 천
1,000,000 .... baek man	백 만
1,100,000 .... baek sib man	백 십 만
2,300,000 .... i baek sam sib man	이 백 삼 십 만
10,000,000 .... cheon man	천 만

One important verb to know is "imnida" which means "to be." To make this a question, change the ending "da" to "ka" as in "imnika."

How much is it? .... Eolma imnikka? 얼 마 입 니 까?
It is 2,000 won. ... I cheon won imnida. 이 천 원 입 니 다

6.8 Restaurants

A basic list of food and beverages which visitors may want to try is provided below.

water .... mul 물
coffee .... keopi 커 피
green tea .... nok cha 녹 차
beer .... maekju 맥 주
soju .... soju 소 주
ramyon .... ramyeon 라 면
kimchi stew .... kimchi jjigae 김 치 찌 개
soy bean stew...dwoen jang jjigae 된 장 찌 개
octopus stew...nakkchi bokkeum 낚 지 볶 음
raw seafood .... woe 회
kalbi .... galbi 갈 비
bulgogi .... bulgogi 불 고 기
garlic .... maneul 마 늘
cooked rice .... bap 밥
California roll .... kimbap 김 밥
fried rice .... bokkeum bap 볶 음 밥

To call a waiter or waitress in a restaurant, say one of three things.

If it is an older woman, say: ... ajumeoni 아 주 머 니
If it is a young woman, say:.......... agassi 아 가 씨
If it is a man, say: .... ajeossi 아 저 씨

To ask for something in a restaurant, just say:

Waitress, can I have some water please?

Ajumeoni, mul chusaeyo?   아 주 머 니, 물 주 세 요

6.9 Signs

Here is a list of a few important signs that you will see in Korea. The old Romanized form *(in italics)* is still common both on signs and in histories and guide books. *(See page 84.)*

Seoul .... 서 울

Busan *(Pusan)* .... 부 산

Daegu *(Taegu)* .... 대 구

Incheon *(Inchon)* .... 인 천

Gwangju *(Kwangju)* .. 광 주

Daejeon *(Taejon)* .... 대 전

Ulsan .... 울 산

drug store .... yak 약

men's toilet .... namja hwajang sil 남 자 화 장 실

women's toilet .... yeoja hwajang sil 여 자 화 장 실

university .... hakgyo 대 학 교

hagwan .... hagwan 학 원

yeogwan .... yeogwan 여 관

police station .... gyeong chal seo 경 찰 서

train station .... yeok 역

subway station .... jeon cheol yeok 전 철 역

bus station .... beo seu teo mi nal 버 스 터 미 날

hospital .... byeong won 병 원

bank .... eun heang 은 행

airport .... gong hang 공 항

6.10 Studying Korean

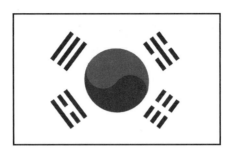

To live comfortably in Korea, expats need to speak some Korean. Otherwise, the most basic yet important tasks can become a drudgery. The ability to speak Korean fluently is not necessary. Rather, foreigners should be able to speak, read, and understand "survival Korean," a basic level of comprehension which enables visitors to take a taxi, read street signs, and discuss money matters in a store or bank.

There are several ways to study Hangul in Korea. Most bookstores have English-Korean dictionaries and a few book and tape sets for sale. One publication by Seoul National University called *Korean Through English* is useful, but there are many others. Some universities, colleges, and private language institutes offer Korean conversation classes to foreigners, though the tuition can be expensive. Many programs located in Seoul are advertised in the English newspapers. Outside the capital, you may have to ask a Korean friend to find one for you.

An economical option is to find a Korean friend and offer to exchange languages for free: you teach them English and they teach you Korean. A large percentage of Korean adults who study English would be happy to have this kind of arrangement. If you cannot find a suitable partner, the English newspapers often carry classified ads from Koreans looking for foreigners interested in a language exchange.